Level 2
Teacher's Resource Book

Barry Scholes and Gill Atha

Collins Educational

Contents

First published in 1989 by Holmes McDougall Ltd., Edinburgh.

This edition published in 1991 by Collins Educational, London and Glasgow.

Reprinted 1992, 1993

ISBN 0 00 314344 9
© Collins Educational, 1991

Printed in Gt. Britain by Antony Rowe Ltd.

Collins Educational

Introduction

Outline of the course:

Level	Age	Pupil's Book	Listening Skills Cassettes	Computer Software (Adventures in English)
Starter	5+	Starter Masters	Starter Cassette	————
		Starter Workbooks		————
Approach	6-7	Approach Book	Approach Cassette	*Goblin Winter*
Level 1	7-8	Book 1	Level 1 Cassette	*Spooky Towers*
Level 2	8-9	Book 2	Level 2 Cassette	*Spellbound*
Level 3	9-10	Book 3	Level 3 Cassette	*Pirate's Treasure*
Level 4	10-11	Book 4	Level 4 Cassette	*Wrecker's Rock*
Level 5	11-12	Book 5	Level 5 Cassette	*McGinty's Gold*

The National Curriculum and English Alive

National Curriculum	Key Stage 1		Key Stage 2				
	Level 1	Level 2	Level 3		Level 4		Level 5
English Alive	Starter	Approach	Level 1	Level 2	Level 3	Level 4	Level 5
Adventures in English		Goblin Winter	Spooky Towers	Spell-bound	Pirate's Treasure	Wrecker's Rock	McGinty's Gold

English Alive is a complete Primary English course in seven levels, covering the age range 5+ to 12+. It has been designed with full regard to the National Curriculum, the *Bullock Report* and to recent thinking on the teaching of language. It is carefully and systematically structured to develop the full range of English skills: speaking, listening, reading and writing and the study of language.

These skills are developed within the context of carefully chosen themes which link language development with other areas of the curriculum and offer wide scope for a variety of follow-up work. The literary extracts which provide the stimuli for many of these themes have been selected to extend the experience of the children.

The course begins in the Infant Department with photocopiable Starter sheets, and three Starter Workbooks. An Approach Book of fourteen units then leads on to the main part of the programme in Books 1-5.

Each level is supported by the Teacher's Resource Book which contains a wealth of follow-up work in the form of photocopiable masters and ideas for the teacher to develop. There is also an audio cassette which provides a structured approach to the development of listening skills. Each tape links with photocopiable masters in the Resource Book.

Also available is the *Adventures in English* series of computer programs. Each adventure links with one of the books and is accompanied by Pressure-fax Spiritmaster activity sheets which provide a variety of stimulating follow-up work.

Aims of the course:
The course aims to provide **the children** with the opportunity to:
- widen ability and experience in reading, writing, listening and speaking.
- link the work done in English to work covered in other disciplines so that the learning that takes place is relevant and meaningful.
- foster in themselves an appreciation and enjoyment of many kinds of literature: stories, prose (factual and fiction), plays, poems etc.
- examine and interpret a wide range of stimuli (familiar and new) — literary,

visual and aural — and to react in a variety of ways to these stimuli i.e. through written work, debate, drama etc.

- work individually in groups on a variety of projects (written and oral) as stimulated by this wide range of stimuli.
- gain increasing clarity in oral and written expression, both factual and creative.
- gain an increased sense of oral and written language for different purposes.

The course aims to provide the teacher with:

- a pupil profile to record pupil's work, progress and mastery of skills. The profile is cross referenced to the attainment targets of the National Curriculum of England and Wales. (See page 129).

- a complete and balanced language course which develops the whole range of language skills and is firmly based on the National Curriculum, the *Bullock Report* and recent thinking.

- a thematic approach to language teaching which is organised to link with other areas of the curriculum; reinforcing the work and giving it meaning and purpose.

- a thorough, colourful and attractive way of presenting children with a variety of resources — literary, visual and aural — to stimulate and encourage their knowledge and appreciation of the language, its structure and how it can be used most effectively.

Level 2

The material in Book 2 is organised into fifteen four-page thematic units. Each unit, together with the supplementary material and follow-up suggestions in the Teacher's Resource Book, offers two weeks' language work.

Unit Structure
The stimulus for each unit is an extract from a children's book, a poem, or factual material in a variety of forms.

The poems and extracts have been selected with regard to their quality, the thoughts and feelings of the writers, and their appeal to children. A wide variety of writing styles and subject matter is represented. The comprehensive range of factual material is designed to help in the development of study skills, logical deduction and judgement. Such skills will link to other subjects across the curriculum.

Each unit is completed by activities to develop language and writing skills.

Notes and Masters
The teacher's notes and photocopiable masters in this Resource Book are intended to complement and extend each unit. They are grouped together, unit by unit, for easy reference.

It is left to the discretion of the teacher which of the masters is appropriate to any child or group. Some of the masters have been designed to give further practice material for the slow learner; others extend the language skills and are appropriate to the more able child. Our aim has been to provide a variety of masters to suit the ability range found in most classrooms.

Certain masters have been designated Skillmasters. Each Skillmaster provides clear explanation and graded practice for a specific skill. It may be kept by the pupils as a permanent reference sheet. Skillmasters are especially useful where a child has a specific difficulty. Those from Level 2 may be used to reinforce later levels of *English Alive*, or indeed any English scheme. Skillmasters from Level 1 will be helpful where revision practice is required.

Also included are specially written group prediction stories and Assessment Masters for use at the end of Level 2 to test progress. In addition to the masters there are suggestions for the development of speaking skills, and a range of follow-up work to link language skills to the rest of the curriculum.

Level 2 Listening Skills Cassette
Each level of English Alive has a Listening Skills cassette which together with the associated activity sheets provides for a carefully structured development of listening skills.

All instructions for the children are recorded on the tape to allow them to work independently. Photocopiable masters which can be made into pupils' self-marking answer cards appear in the Appendices, together with a contents list for the cassette.

Pupil Profile

English Alive is cross-referenced to the National Curriculum of England and Wales, and the attainment target for each activity is clearly identified throughout the Resource Books: e.g. **AT3/3b** refers to Attainment Target 3, Level 3b. The pupil's work, progress and mastery of these skills may be recorded using the Pupil Profile found on page 116. Any method of recording may be used: e.g. shading, ticking, ringing, etc. Mastery of a particular attainment target may be indicated by an appropriate marking of the attainment target heading.

In addition to the profile there is a sheet which the children may use to keep a simple record of their progress.

Level 2 Book: Contents

Level 2 Masters: Contents

Unit 1

Time — A Martian Comes to Stay
Theme — Visitor from Space
Stimulus — *A Martian Comes to Stay* from *Uninvited Ghosts* by Penelope Lively, Heinemann.

AT1 Speaking/listening
3a & descriptions from the point of
c-d view of a Martian
3c selecting ten objects to be taken back to Mars as typical of our life on Earth

ATs 1-4 Word skills
● nouns — classification
— attributes
● crossword: outer space words

AT2 Reading
3b-e inference, speculation
3b; d cloze procedure
context clues
3f diagram of a bicycle

AT3 Writing
3a sentence building:
— completing sentences
— sentences about nouns
3a & d — sentences about the parts of a bicycle
3d descriptions of everyday things explaining the rules of a sport
3b-c & imaginative — a Martian visits
e the classroom
— a trip in a flying saucer
3d designing and writing about Martian clothes, homes, food, money etc.

Cloze passage:
The actual words used by the author in this extract are given here for reference purposes only. They should not be regarded as the correct answers — 1) lived 2) vegetables 3) with 4) Gran 5) what 6) happened.

Activity sheets:
2.1a sentences, making sense (Skillmaster) **AT3/3a**
2.1b sentences, personal facts **AT3/3a**
2.1c descriptions from the point of view of a Martian **AT2/3d; AT3/3d**
2.1d animal fact sheet (vocabulary and reference) **AT1/3a & d; AT3/3b-d**

Listening skills: AT1/3a & d; AT3/3c-d
2.1e aural memory — recalling detail

Side 1, track 1 Tape Counter _____
This track features two eye-witness accounts of the sighting of a flying saucer. Each child should listen to the tape BEFORE being given the activity sheet. They are then presented with multi-choice answers to test their recall of the facts.

The correct answers are: 1) **a** 2) **b** 3) **a** 4) **a** 5) **b** 6) **a** 7) **b** 8) **a** 9) **a** 10) **a**.

Also on the sheet are further activities:
— drawing the saucer, as described **AT1/3d; AT2/3d**
— re-telling the events in pupil's own words **AT1/3a; AT3/3b-c**
— speculation on what might happen next **AT3/3c**

Speaking and listening:
1 *Aliens.* Two or three children pretend to be creatures from an alien world. The other children then ask them questions about their life and planet. **AT1/3a & c**

2 *Twenty Questions.* The aliens invent a 'Martian' noun and then answer twenty questions about it. **AT1/3d**

3 *Where Are You Going?* — an alphabet game. Each child has to invent a sentence which answers the question 'Where are you going?' Each sentence must feature as many words as possible beginning with the same letter. The next player moves to the next letter in the alphabet. **AT1/3c & d**
e.g. I am going to Australia to ask Aunty Alice about animals.
I am going to Birmingham to blow up a big blue balloon.
I am going to Mars to make Martians munch mountains of macaroni.
I am going to Zambia to zoom over zebras in a zoo.

4 *Classification.* Divide the class into teams and ask them in turn to provide class names for a variety of things.
e.g. Venus, Mars, Jupiter and Saturn are all ____?
What is one word for the things we eat? etc. etc. **AT1/3d**

5 *Odd-Man-Out.* A variation of the classification game where one word does not belong.
e.g. sun moon cloud star planet
apple potato orange banana

peach **AT1/3d**

6 Explain as if to a Martian how to do simple everyday things like tying a shoe lace, making a cup of tea etc. **AT1/3a-b, d**

7 Act what happens when an alien knocks at the door. **AT1/3d**

Follow-up activities:

1 Make a model of an alien landscape using papier maché. Add buildings and different forms of transport.

2 Make a life-size painting of Quogg the Martian.

3 Make a frieze showing a creature, its pet and its spacecraft for every planet in our solar system. (Science **AT16**)

4 Make a frieze showing the history of space exploration.

5 Find out about the planets of our solar system. Make a fact sheet, and add drawings and photographs. (Science **AT16**); **AT2/3f; AT3/3d**

6 Use the personal data from the fact sheet 2.1b to make bar charts or pictograms. **AT3/3d**; (Maths **AT13/3a**); (Science **AT1/3f & g**).

7 Use 'What is a Sentence?' from the *Adventures in English* series of computer programs (Collins Educational). This program has three parts. The first part shows that sentences must make complete sense, the second that they must be properly punctuated and the third is a test. The learning responses are monitored by the computer and the child is given practice appropriate to his needs. A full profile of his progress can be displayed if the teacher requires it.

'What is a Sentence?' is available together with 'Some Common Confusions' on a single disc. For more details of the *Adventures in English* series please see the appendices. **AT3/3a**

8 Poems: **AT2/3a**
'The Alien' — Julie Holder
'The Mystery Creatures' — Wes Magee
(Both are in *A Third Poetry Book*, Oxford)
'On Some Other Planet' — John Rice
'At the Housefly Planet' — Christian Morgenstern
'The Owl and the Astronaut' — Gareth Owen
'Shed in Space' — Gareth Owen
(All four are in *The Kingfisher Book of Comic Verse*)
'Spaceways' — *An Anthology of Space Poems* — John Foster, O.U.P.

9 *Process writing:* **AT3/3e; AT4/3d**
Many teachers now use process writing in their language lessons. English Alive is an ideal complement to this approach, offering a wealth of ideas for children to explore. Unit **2.1** for example provides four different writing activities in both expressive and transactional forms.

What is Process Writing?
Process writing is a recent development in children's writing. It has been highly successful in America and Australia, and is now showing equal success in this country.

Process writing involves writing in successive drafts, shaping and reshaping ideas until the writer is satisfied with the content. In the later drafts serious proof reading takes place and the surface features of writing — spelling and punctuation — are improved to the best of the writer's ability.

The final stage of the writing process comes when the writer decides, with the help of the teacher, that his work is ready to be presented to a reader. The best way is to publish it, either as part of a class book or as a book in its own right. In this form it may achieve library status and provide continuing pleasure and inspiration to others.

Writing in drafts has several advantages:
- It encourages a professional approach to writing, allowing the child to express himself without the need to get everything right first time.
- It allows him to review his writing in conference with teacher, friend or peer group. Research has shown that children who help others improve their work find it much easier to improve their own.
- It gives opportunities to re-think ideas and to reorganise material. In doing so the child will develop a greater understanding of the writing process.
- It places spelling and punctuation into perspective, secondary to the expression of ideas.

- It shows that spelling and punctuation are nevertheless very important to the clear presentation of ideas, because errors detract from the meaning and make communication with the reader more difficult.

Correcting errors:
It is important in process writing that the teacher should not mark the work in a conventional way. As far as possible the children should learn to find and correct their own errors. The teacher's role is to help them to do so.

One way is to ask the children to circle any words they feel may be spelt incorrectly and to underline any expressions they feel could be improved, or where they are unsure of punctuation. A dictionary and a short conference with the teacher may then be all that is needed to make substantial improvements.

Although process writing involves little or no marking in the conventional sense, its demands on the teacher's time are considerable. The teacher needs to keep up to date with each stage of each pupil's writing and be ready to give help as required. The publication stage will involve preparing material for the pupils to make their own books, preferably with hard covers. A fully professional product will require typing or word processing the manuscript. The purchase of a word processor program or ROM for the school computer is strongly recommended. Older children will enjoy typing their final drafts on a word processor.

To those teachers who feel that process writing demands a great deal of their time we can say that they are perfectly right — it does! But the rewards are great for both pupil and teacher.

To those teachers who feel that process writing takes away their control of the pupil's writing again we can say that it does, but it places that control where it rightly belongs — in the hands of the writer.

Book List

Graves, D. (1983) *Writing: Teachers and Children at Work* (Heinemann)

Newman, J. (1984) *The Craft of Children's Writing* (Scholastic)

Newman, J. (Ed.) (1985) *Whole Language, Theory in Use* (Scholastic)

Moon, C. (Ed.) (1985) *Practical Ways to Teach Writing* (Ward Lock)

Clay, M. (1975) *What Did I Write: Beginning Writing Behaviour* (Heinemann)

Henderson, E. H. & Beers, J. W. (Eds.) (1980) *Developmental and Cognitive Aspects of Learning to Spell: A Reflection of Word Knowledge* (I.R.A.)

Henderson, E. H. (1981) *Learning to Read and Spell: The Child's Knowledge of Words* (Northern Illinois University Press)

Newkirk, T. & Atwell, N. (Eds.) (1982) *Understanding Writing: Ways of Observing Learning and Teaching* (North West Regional Exchange, U.S.A.)

Sentences Always Make Sense

A sentence must make complete sense. It should say something about a person or thing. Find the six complete sentences below and tick them.

1 Kuldip is never late for school.
2 We are going to.
3 after twelve o'clock.
4 Joanne lives next to Sue.
5 My favourite.
6 Dad has bought a new car.

7 John broke.
8 We play football every day.
9 Rakesh saw a flying saucer.
10 as fast as he could.
11 Mr Dobson was.
12 Katy is painting a picture.

Add more words to the remaining six to make them into good sentences.

1 _____

2 _____

3 _____

4 _____

5 _____

6 _____

Name_____

Hello Earthling, my name is Quogg.
I wonder if you would be so good
as tell me something about yourself?

About Me

Please answer these questions about yourself.
Answer in complete sentences.

1 What is your name? _____

2 Where do you live? _____

_____

3 What kind of house do you live in? _____

_____

4 Who else lives in your house? _____

_____

5 What pets do you have? _____

_____

6 What is your favourite sport? _____

_____

7 What is your favourite T.V. programme? _____

_____

8 What is your favourite book? _____

_____

9 Which school do you go to? _____

_____

10 What is your favourite lesson? _____

2.1b Sentences — personal fact sheet
© Collins Educational 1990. AT3/3a

Name_____

ENGLISH
ALIVE

Level 2
Master

2.1c

Descriptions

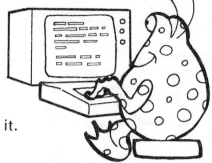

Quogg is writing his report on life on Earth as he sees it.
Can you work out what he is describing?

1   These are boxes made of metal and sheets of glass. People get in them and sit
down. The box begins to make a noise. It then moves away on four wheels. When
it reaches a different place it stops again and becomes quiet. The people then get
out again and walk away.

They call this box a _____ .

2   This is a box which people have in their homes. The box talks to them. One side of
the box lights up and the people stare at it for long periods. Sometimes they laugh
at it.

They call this box a _____ .

3   This object looks something like an Earth person, but it is not alive. It wears old
clothes. Children sometimes use it to collect money. Then they grow tired of it
and burn it on a big fire.

It is called a _____ .

How do you think Quogg would describe the things below? Choose *two* of them and
write his description.

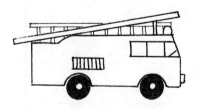

a fire engine   a supermarket trolley   an elephant   a disco

_____

_____

_____

_____

2.1c Descriptions
© Collins Educational 1990. AT2/3d; AT3/3d

Name_____

Earth Animals

Please complete this fact sheet on Earth animals. Add any others you know of.

Animal	Description	Home	Food	Movement	Sound
	Two arms, two legs. About 2m tall. walks upright.	House, flat etc.	Meat, fish, fruit, vegetables	walks	talks
				ambles	
			meat		
			fruit		
				gallops	
					bleats
		kennel			
		web			

2.1d Animals — fact sheet
© Collins Educational 1990. AT2/3i; AT3/3d

Name_____

ENGLISH
ALIVE

Level 2
Master

2.1e

U.F.O.

First listen to the two eye-witness accounts on track 1, side 1 of the Level 2 listening skills cassette.

Then answer the questions below.
Each question has two answers, but only *one* tells what the witnesses really said.
Underline each correct answer.

1. Farmer Brown was
   a) ploughing a field
   b) mending his tractor

2. He was blinded for a moment by
   a) a bright red light
   b) a bright orange light

3. He heard a
   a) loud humming sound
   b) loud buzzing sound

4. The bright light was followed by
   a) five small red lights
   b) five small green lights

5. His feet began to
   a) tingle
   b) lift off the ground

6. The tractor began to
   a) shake
   b) lift off the ground

7. At the end
   a) he was carried off by the saucer
   b) he fell to the ground

8. P.C. Buckley was
   a) going north
   b) going south

9. P.C. Buckley said the saucer had
   a) what seemed like portholes
   b) bright, silver lights

10. The saucer was
    a) more than 25 metres in diameter
    b) less than 25 metres in diameter

Now draw what you think the saucer might have looked like.

On a separate sheet of paper tell what happened to Farmer Brown and P.C. Buckley. Make up your own ending to the story.

Unit 2

Title — Double Trouble
Theme — Pairs and Myself
Stimuli — from *The Emma Dilemma* by Catherine Sefton (Faber); *I Did a Bad Thing Once* by Allan Ahlberg, from *Please Mrs. Butler* (Kestrel).

AT1 Speaking/listening
3a & c projection
3a & c reporting on experience

ATs 1-4 Word skills
● association — words which go together
● word steps — 3 letter words, using clues

AT2 Reading
3b-e   checking facts
3b; d cloze procedure
3d   discussing poem
3f   alphabetical order to 3rd letter
3f   skimming to spot errors in alphabetical order

AT3 Writing
3a   question sentences
3b-c & e   imaginative story, writer as participant
3c   personal writing
3d   writing a poem using a plan

AT4 Spelling
3a   homophones — through/threw; write/right; knew/new; blue/blew; there/their; wood/would; by/buy; see/sea

Cloze passage
The actual words used by the author in this extract are given here for reference purposes only. They should not be regarded as the 'correct' answers — 1) on 2) before 3) dream 4) confused 5) said 6) me 7) There 8) a 9) about.

Activity sheets:
2.2a   plurals: *f* to *ve*; *-oes*, *-os* (Skillmaster) **AT4/3b**
2.2b   question sentences (Skillmaster) **AT3/3a**
2.2c   word puzzles **ATs 1-4**

Listening skills: Side 1, track 2. Tape counter _____
2.2d   auditory/visual association — matching spoken words to pictures.

The listener has to decide which of the five house painters on the activity sheet fits the spoken description.
(The correct painter is the one in the middle). **AT1/3d; AT2/3c**

Listening and speaking:
1 Aural Cloze. Read or tell a story, missing out words as appropriate. Aural cloze gives opportunity to monitor the responses of the children and to make appropriate modifications as the reading continues. **AT1/3c & d**

2 Asking questions. Three useful games for developing the art of asking appropriate questions are: What's My Line?, Twenty Questions and Famous People. In the latter one child pretends to be a celebrity from the present, or a famous (or infamous!) person from history. **AT1/3b, c & d**

3 Present the children with an everyday object. They then have to think of different uses for the object, apart from the obvious one. For example, the children may think a book has only one use, but it may be used as a step to reach a high shelf, a weight to press flowers, a sight screen for private work etc. etc. **AT1/3c**

4 When the children have examined a number of objects in this way, ask them to tell a story about an object and how it is used in unusual ways. **AT1/3c & d**

5 Choral speech: All these poems are suitable for choral speech:
'I Wonder Why Dad is So Thoroughly Mad' — Jack Prelutsky from *The New Kid on the Block* (Greenwillow Books)
'Chivvy' — Michael Rosen, from *You Tell Me* (Puffin)
'I'm the Youngest in Our House' — Michael Rosen, from *Wouldn't You Like to Know* (Andre Deutsch)
'Orders of the Day' — John Cunliffe, included in *A Second Poetry Book* (Oxford) **AT1/3d**

6 Talk about two or more sides to a personality. What brings out the worst in people? Discuss occasions when the children have shown their worst sides, losing their tempers for example. Act out any suitable incidents. Look for ways in which the situation could have had a different ending, perhaps if someone had behaved differently.

AT1/3a & c.

Poems which will be useful are:

'The Quarrel' — Eleanor Jargeon, from *A First Poetry Book* (Oxford)

'The Rebel Child' — Leslie Norris, from *A Fourth Poetry Book* (Oxford)

'Growing Up' — Gareth Owen, from *A Second Poetry Book* (Oxford)

'Myself' — Edgar A. Guest, included in *Poetry Plus 5* (Schofield & Sims)

7 Tone of voice: Try acting the incidents from 6 above in different tones of voice. What effect does this have on the situation? Try saying angry words in a friendly way. **AT1/3c & d**

Follow-up activities:

1 Alphabetical Order: Make an alphabetical list of the telephone numbers of friends, neighbours, school, doctor, parent's place of work etc. **AT3/3d**

2 Make an illustrated class book of paired words: high and low, lock and key, odds and ends, high and dry, rough and tumble etc. **AT3/3d**

3 Use 'Some Common Confusions', the homophones computer program in the *Adventures in English* series (Holmes McDougall). This program explains the differences between homophones, tests the children's understanding of them and gives further help if needed. The homophones covered are:

there and their; wood and would; write and right; by and buy; where and wear.

'Some Common Confusions' is available together with 'What is a Sentence?' on a single disc. For more details of the *Adventures in English* series please refer to the appendices. **ATs1-4; AT4/3a**

Computer program listings:

Below are two simple computer programs to develop the use of alphabetical order. **AT2/3e**

Please note:

The children will need to have learned the alphabet before using the programs.

Both programs have been written for the BBC range of computers, but can be modified to run on other machines. If either of the programs should fail to run correctly, please check the listing for keying-in errors. The listings are very simple and capable of considerable improvement. The user is invited to make any modifications he wishes.

Which Letter Comes Next?

This program gives practice in alphabetical order.

Lines 2-6 may be omitted. The program runs as follows:

The program	Line nos.
Screen Mode 7 is selected.	10
A random number is generated to determine the random letter.	20
The child is then asked the question, "Which letter comes after" (the random letter)?	30
The main input routine.	40-110
Line 50 forces lower case input of the child's answer. This is	50
then checked.	70
If the answer is wrong the message "Wrong. Press space bar" is given, and a new answer asked for.	80-110
If the answer is correct the child is rewarded with the message "Good. Press space bar for next letter".	120-140
The computer then selects a new number, and the program continues.	20

```
 2  REM WHICH LETTER COMES NEXT?
 4  REM B. SCHOLES 1988
10  MODE 7
20  X=RND(25)+96
30  PRINTTAB(4,12)"Which letter comes
    after";CHR$130;CHR$(X);CHR$135;"?"
40  REPEAT
50  *FX202,48
60  INPUTTAB(16,14),ANS$
70  IF ASC(ANS$)=X+1 GOTO110
80  PRINTTAB(6,14)"Wrong. Press space
    bar."
90  A=GET
100 PRINTTAB(4,14)SPC(30)
110 UNTIL ASC(ANS$)=X+1
120 PRINTTAB(0,18)"Good. Press space bar
    for next letter."
130 A=GET
140 CLS:GOTO20
```

Which letter comes first?

This program also gives practice in alphabetical order.

Lines 2-6 may be omitted. The program runs as follows:

The Program	Line nos.
Screen Mode 7 is selected.	10
A random number is generated to determine the first letter.	20
The second letter is selected and checked to see if it is different from the first letter.	50
The computer then checks which letter comes first and stores this letter as L$.	40-50
The child is then asked which letter comes first.	60
The main input routine.	70-140
Line 80 forces lower case input of the child's answer.	80-90
The answer is checked against L$.	100
If the answer is wrong, the child is told so and asked for another answer.	110-140
If the answer is correct an appropriate message is given and the computer generates two further letters.	150-170
	20-50

```
  2  REM FIRST LETTER
  4  REM B.SCHOLES 1988
 10  MODE 7
 20  X=RND(25)+96
 30  REPEAT:Y=RND(25)+96:UNTIL Y<>X
 40  IF X<Y THEN L$=CHR$(X)
 50  IF X>Y THEN L$=CYR$(Y)
 60  PRINTTAB(1,12)"Which  letter  comes
     first ";CHR$130;CHR$(X);CHR$135; "or";
     CHR$130; CHR$(Y); CHR$135; "?"
 70  REPEAT
 80  *FX202,48
 90  INPUTTAB(16,14),AN$
100  IF AN$=L$ GOTO140
110  PRINTTAB(3,14)"Wrong.  Press  space
     bar."
120  A=GET
130  PRINTTAB(3,14)SPC(30)
140  UNTIL AN$=L$
150  PRINTTAB(0,18)"Good. Press space bar
     for next letter."
160  A=GET
170  CLS:GOTO20
```

Name_____

ENGLISH
ALIVE

Level 2
Master

2.2a

More Than One

To make a word more than one we usually add **-s**.

| boy, boys   girl, girls |

When a word ends in **-f** we change the **-f** to **-ve** before adding **-s**.

| loaf, loa**ves**   half, hal**ves**   life, li**ves** |

Make each of these words more than one.

leaf _____   shelf _____   knife _____   calf _____

wolf _____   elf _____   self _____   scarf _____

thief _____   wife _____

Choose five of these new words and write a sentence for each one.

1 _____

2 _____

3 _____

4 _____

5 _____

If a word ends in a consonant and **-o**, we add **-es** to make more than one.

tomato   tomato**es**   volcano   _____

potato   potato**es**   hero   _____

echo   _____   torpedo   _____

With some words we just add **-s**.

| pianos   solos |

Label these pictures.

2.2a Skillmaster — plurals
© Collins Educational 1990. AT4/3b

Name_____

Questions

A question sentence begins with a capital letter and ends in a question mark.
Arrange these words to make good question sentences.

1 is Jane where _____

2 do where live you _____

3 this his coat is _____

4 go bed when you to do _____

5 John is why crying _____

Write the questions for which these are the answers. The first one has been done for you.

1 I live at 21 Church Road. | Where do you live? |

2 I am nine years old. _____

3 I go to Green Lane School. _____

4 My favourite lesson is English. _____

5 School ends at half past three. _____

6 I have my tea at four o'clock. _____

7 I have a little kitten. _____

8 We are going to Spain. _____

2.2b Skillmaster — question sentences
© Collins Educational 1990. AT3/3a

Word Puzzles

Complete these word steps, using the clues to help you.

1 Opposite to ill

2 Not yet found

3 Players on the same side

4 It lives underground

5 Found in birds' nests

6 Opposite to hard

7 Opposite to fat

Provide your own clues for these word steps.

1 To tear

2 _____

3 _____

4 _____

5 _____

6 _____

7 _____

Change one word into another by changing only one letter at a time.
Use the clues to help you.

cup

do this with a knife

a pet

bat

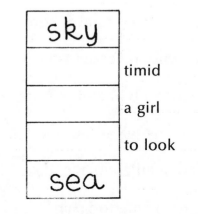

sky

timid

a girl

to look

sea

Name_____

The Real Mr. Rudge

When you know which is the real Mr. Rudge, write a description of him.

_____

_____

_____

_____

_____

_____

_____

_____

2.2d Auditory/visual association
© Collins Educational 1990. **AT1/3d; AT2/3c**

Unit 3

Title — Spellbound
Theme — Witches
Stimuli — from *Maggie Gumption* by Margaret Stuart Barry Hutchinson Junior Books Ltd.; *Witch Goes Shopping* by Lillian Moore from *See My Little Poison Ivy*, (New York: Atheneum. Included in *A First Poetry Book*, Oxford

AT1 Speaking/listening
3c-d   making up spells and rhymes

ATs 1-4 Word skills
- adjectives
- vocabulary: nouns beginning with "b" shopping words (supermarket)
- classification
- alliteration

AT2 Reading
3b-c & f   reading for the main idea
3b-e   literal/inferential/speculative
3f   scanning
3f   checking facts
3f   alphabetical order — 4th letter
3f   skimming picture for details

AT3 Writing
3a   exclamations
3b-c & e   choosing a spell from the contents page of a witch's spellbook, writing the spell and the recipe, and a story about how it works
3b-c & e   writing an eye-witness account of the witch's visit to a supermarket
3c   using description as introduction to a story
3d   spells and rhymes
3d   descriptions using adjectives
3d   making a warning poster
3d   making a special offer poster
3d   designing a food label

Activity sheets:
2.3a   writing a poem using an outline **AT3/3d, ATs 1-4**
2.3b   Supermarket game — the board and rules **AT1/3c-e**
2.3c   Supermarket Game — the shopping lists **AT1/3c-e**

2.3d   group prediction *Mrs. Canby's Cottage* — 1 **AT1/3c; AT2/3c-e**
2.3e   group prediction *Mrs. Canby's Cottage* — 2 **AT1/3c, AT2/3c-e**
2.3f   group prediction *Mrs. Canby's Cottage* — 3 **AT1/3c; AT2/3c-e**
2.3g   group prediction *Mrs. Canby's Cottage* — 4 **AT1/3c, AT2/3c-e**

Notes:
2.3a   Writing a poem using an outline
This sheet provides an outline for writing a simple poem about a witch, her cottage and her cat. The sheet has boxes, arranged like a brick wall for suitable adjectives to be written in.

Although the structure is little more than a list of words and is unlikely to produce many prize-winning poems, its main value is that it will enable the less able children to produce an interesting piece of writing in verse form. Brainstorming will produce a range of adjectives for the children to use and arrange in any order they feel suitable. The poem does not need to rhyme, but if that is preferred the rhyming words can be written in first.

The children may make up their own title for the poem. There is no reason why a fourth verse should not be added. The example below shows what may be achieved.

Witch's Cottage
An old, dark, dusty,
Damp, gloomy, shadowy,
Spooky, sinister, chilling, eerie,
Frightening witch's cottage.

A prowling, sleek, black,
Green-eyed, angry,
Sharp-clawed, arch-backed,
Spitting witch's cat.

An ugly, sharp-eyed,
Hooked-nosed, wrinkled,
Cackling, claw-fingered, warty,
Wicked old witch.

A terrified, screaming, scrambling,
Fleeing, panting, running,
Stumbling, falling, crying, limping,
Sorry little boy.

2.3b and 2.3c Supermarket Game
The Supermarket Game consists of a board and rules (**2.3b**) and six shopping lists (**2.3c**). The only extra equipment needed is a dice and one counter per player. The game gives opportunity to follow instructions, to

find the right shelves by classifying the items on the list, and to use the plan to devise an appropriate route.

A variation is to ask the children to make up lists for other children to use. In this case please remember the items on the list should be arranged randomly. A further possibility would be to include more than one item for a particular shelf, but to place them apart on the shopping list.

For those children with the patience for detailed forward planning, each list could be carefully studied in conjunction with the plan and then rewritten in the order the items will be collected.

After the game the shopping lists could be rewritten in alphabetical order.

2.3d-2.3f Group prediction story — *Mrs. Canby's Cottage*
This is the first of the four specially-written group prediction stories for Level 2. It is in four parts.

What is Group Prediction?
Group prediction is a teacher-led activity developing both thinking and speaking skills. It encourages the children:
a) to examine a text carefully in order to make predictions about its eventual outcome
b) to expose their opinions and defend them when challenged
c) to evaluate critically these predictions and inferences by re-examining the details of the text, both explicit and implicit
d) to modify these predictions as and when appropriate.

Using the Stories:
Experience has shown that the optimum group size is between eight and twelve.

Each part should be read carefully and the questions discussed. Opinions should be expressed, criticised and if necessary modified. Predictions should be made which fit the evidence of the text. There may be several possible outcomes at this stage. When reasoned predictions have been made, the next part of the story may be read. This could follow directly in the same session or saved for another lesson. After a careful reading of the last part children will be able to assess how close they were to the outcome of the story. It may well be that none of their predictions is close to its actual development. However, as long as their predictions have

been carefully reasoned from the text, they may be equal, or indeed superior, to the writer's ending. Group prediction is therefore very useful in developing children's ideas about writing stories.

A re-examination of the earlier text is encouraged at the end of each story. This allows the children to spot missed clues, comment on any red herrings and examine mistaken inferences. This is even more useful if the teacher has made tape-recordings of the earlier sessions.

Speaking and listening skills:
1   Shopping Game: The teacher names a specialist shop e.g. greengrocers saying "I went to the greengrocer's and bought some onions." Succeeding players choose another item from his stock. Those who cannot think of a suitable one drop out.

This can also be made into a memory game by repeating the entire list before adding a new item.   **AT1/3a, c & d**

2   Act out going into different shops to buy things.   **AT1/3d**

3   Make and record a group story about a witch. The group should begin with a stimulus such as a bottle from the witch's cupboard, an old key, or a broomstick. The stimulus may also be a given situation e.g. trapped, like Marion, in a witch's cottage (**2.3d-2.3f**) or as in the computer program 'Spellbound' (see following notes).

The group then discuss possible lines of story development. When a storyline has been worked out it can be recorded on tape along with sound effects. The children will need to experiment with these before the recording of the story. **AT1/3a, c & d**

4   Fortune Teller: One child makes up a fortune for another child by reading his palm, the bumps on his head or the lines on his face.   **AT1/3d**

Follow-up activities:
1   Use a projector to cast shadows on a wall or a screen. Practise making witch-like shadows. Alternatively make shadow puppets.

2   Make a life-size model of a witch with a broomstick.

3   Spells: The teacher as witch, or wizard,

turns the entire class into cats, snakes, robots etc. and they have to move about the room in the appropriate manner. **AT1/3d**

4   Make a collection of exclamations from comics, advertisements etc. **ATs 1-4**

5   Make advertisements for the items witches would buy e.g. cauldrons, wands, magic ingredients, broomsticks, hats and cloaks etc. **AT3/3d**

Computer program listing:
Secret letter **AT2/3f**
This program uses the children's knowledge of alphabetical order. The pupil has to guess the letter selected randomly by the computer. The search narrows with each reasonable guess, and the children will be encouraged to devise an efficient search strategy.

The program has been written for the BBC range of computers, but can be modified to run on other machines.

Please note:
If the program does not run correctly please check for the listing for keying-in errors.

The program as presented here is very simple and the user is invited to make any improvements he wishes.

Lines 2-6 may be omitted. The program runs as follows:

The program	Line nos.
Screen mode 7 is selected.	10
The computer uses numbers to generate letters. The lowest number (LOW) is set to represent "a" and HIGH represents "z".	20
The message "I am thinking of a letter between a and z." is shown on screen.	30-40
The computer generates a random number.	50
This is converted to a number which will represent a suitable letter.	60
The main input routine.	70-150
Lower case entry is forced.	90
The pupil enters a guess.	100
The answer is then checked and the numbers HIGH and LOW modified as appropriate.	110-130
A new range of letters is then displayed.	140

When the letter is identified a message is displayed on screen, and the player is asked to press the space bar.
The program then begins again.   160-180

```
2    REM SECRET LETTER
4    REM B.SCHOLES 1988
10   MODE 7
20   LOW = 97:HIGH = 122
30   PRINTTAB(1,6)"I am thinking of a
     letter between"
40   FOR Y = 1TO2: PRINTTAB(11,Y+8)
     CHR$141;CHR$134;CHR$(LOW);
     CHR$135;"&";CHR$134; CHR$(HIGH):
     NEXT Y
50   N = RND(26)
60   X = 96+N
70   REPEAT
80   PRINTTAB(17,14)SPC(30)
90   *FX202,48
100  INPUTTAB(16,14),AN$
110  A = ASCAN$
120  IF A>X THEN HIGH = A
130  IF A<X THEN LOW = A
140  FOR Y = TO2: PRINTTAB(11,Y+8)
     CHR$141,CHR$134,CHR$(LOW);
     CHR$135;"&";CHR$134;
     CHR$(HIGH):NEXT Y
150  UNTIL AN$ = CHR$(X)
160  CLS: FOR Y = 1TO2:PRINTTAB(0,Y+8)
     CHR$141; "Well done. The secret
     letter was ";CHR$136;CHR$(X);".": NEXT
     Y
170  PRINT TAB(12,13) "Press space bar"
180  A = GET:RUN
```

Spellbound (Collins Educational)
This unit has been designed to introduce the computer adventure program 'Spellbound'. This is the third in the Collins Educational series *Adventures in English*. All the programs in the series provide a stimulating extension of the work covered in the *English Alive* course.

'Spellbound' consists of a computer program and a book of 24 Pressure-fax activity sheets, in which the children attempt to escape from the witch's castle.

Full details of 'Spellbound' and the *Adventures in English* series can be found in the appendices of this book.

Name_____

Writing a Poem

Choose describing words to fit each box. When you have finished you will have written a poem about a witch's cottage, her cat and the witch herself.
Remember: poems do not need to rhyme, but it you want yours to rhyme, choose the rhyming words first.

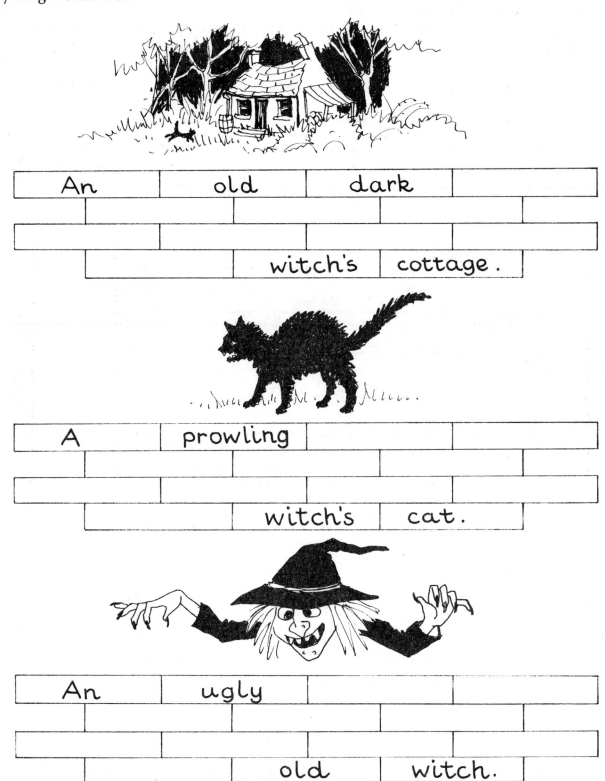

An	old	dark	
		witch's	cottage.

A	prowling		
		witch's	cat.

An	ugly		
		old	witch.

Name_____

Supermarket Game (4-6 players)

You will need: This sheet with the board and rules, the shopping lists from sheet
2.3c, a dice, and a counter for each player.

> **Rules**
> 1 Each player is given a shopping list and a counter.
> 2 He must then move around the supermarket according to the throws of the dice
>   and the sections he needs to visit.
> 3 On arriving at the shelf of his choice he must ask the other players for the item. If
>   all the players agree that he is at the right shelf then the shopper may cross it off
>   his list and move on for his next purchase.
> 4 If he is at the wrong shelf e.g. looking for strawberry jam at the jellies shelf, then
>   he must miss a turn.
> 5 The winner is the first through the checkout with his shopping complete.

 Supermarket Game

Name: _____

Shopping List

- lamb chops
- whipping cream
- chocolate biscuits
- cheese plant
- cornflakes
- frozen peas
- bananas
- toothpaste
- tin of tomato soup
- onions

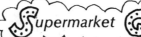 Supermarket Game

Name: _____

Shopping List

- Super Mog cat food
- Dazzler comic
- chicken drumsticks
- toilet rolls
- potatoes
- black cherry yoghurt
- strawberry ice cream
- fresh cream cakes
- melon
- orange squash

Supermarket Game

Name: _____

Shopping List

- Daily News
- sliced loaf
- cheese
- pork chops
- toothbrush
- fish fingers
- apples
- Bow Wow dog food
- cabbage
- rice

Supermarket Game

Name: _____

Shopping List

- pork fillet
- butter
- sprouts
- tin of peaches
- packet of spaghetti
- frozen sausages
- toilet soap
- box of chocolates
- oranges
- muffins

 Supermarket Game

Name: _____

Shopping List

- TV programme guide
- stewing beef
- Supersoft soap
- tea bags
- single cream
- cauliflower
- frozen mixed vegetables
- tuna fish in brine
- kiwi fruit
- digestive biscuits

Supermarket Game

Name: _____

Shopping List

- roast ham
- strawberries
- Curry-Up frozen meal
- air freshener
- tinned carrots
- granary loaf
- leeks
- skimmed milk
- Busy Lizzy plant
- tin of corned beef

2.3c Supermarket game
© Collins Educational 1990. AT3/3d; AT1/3c & d

Mrs. Canby's Cottage
(Part 1)

Long ago, at the edge of the wood,
lived a mother and her daughter, Marion.
One day as Marion was bringing water from
the well a passing traveller gave her a letter for
her mother.

'It's from Mrs. Canby,' said her mother as she began to read it.

'Who is Mrs. Canby?' asked Marion.

'She lives in a cottage in the woods. Your dear departed father and I used to visit her before you were born. Oh, dear! She is ill and needs someone to do the housework until she gets better.' She put down the letter in dismay. 'I can't leave the animals and the crops. What shall we do?'

'Could I go?' Marion asked excitedly.

Mother thought for a long moment, while Marion waited eagerly.

'Only if you promise to take great care in the woods, and to follow the path very carefully.' Marion promised.

The rest of the morning was spent preparing food and presents for Mrs. Canby, and it was early afternoon before Marion was able to set off along the woodland path.

At first the path was easy to follow, but after about half an hour Marion found the woods grew gloomier, and the path was much less used and rather overgrown in places. It was not at all easy to find her way. Then, just when she was beginning to think she was lost, she saw the cottage in a clearing in the wood. Sighing with relief she knocked at the little green door. When no one answered she gently pushed the door open.

The room inside was dusty and Marion knew she would have a lot of cleaning to do.

'Mrs. Canby,' she called pushing open another door, 'Where are you, Mrs. Canby?' She stepped into a very strange room indeed. In the centre of the floor was a huge black cauldron. Marion began to feel deeply afraid. Could Mrs. Canby be a witch?

Suddenly the door behind her slammed shut, and a key turned in the lock.

'Mrs. Canby, it's me, Marion!' she cried in alarm. There was a cruel, cackling laugh from the other side of the door.

'Welcome to my cottage, dear!'

To think and talk about:
1   Do you think it was wise to send Marion alone to Mrs. Canby's cottage?
2   What else might Marion's mother have done?
3   Do you think Mrs. Canby really is a witch?
4   What do you think will happen next? Why?

2.3d   Group prediction — 1
© Collins Educational 1990. AT1/3c; AT2/3c-e

Name_____

Mrs. Canby's Cottage
(Part 2)

The door was securely locked. Marion looked around for a way of escape, but the only windows had bars across them. She decided to examine everything in the room to see if it could help her.

Apart from the cauldron there was an oak table, a three-legged stool and an armchair. One wall was filled with shelves, piled high with dusty objects. In a corner was a locked cupboard. Perhaps there was a key somewhere? Marion put down her basket, and moved across to the shelves. She blew away the dust and wiped aside some long cobwebs. A large black spider scuttled away, but Marion was too used to spiders to give it a second glance.

On the shelves were bottles and jars, some with labels and some without. Marion began to read them: Serpents' Spittle, Bee Stings, Pickled Toads' Tongues, Dragons' Blood, Eyes of Newts, Impossible Powder, Never Known To Fail Magic Mixture, Broomstick-Go-Faster Polish, Surprise Syrup, Demon Dust, and others too faint to read. The top shelf was very high, so Marion stood on the three-legged stool. The shelf was completely empty, except for one thing.

'Now we're getting somewhere!' said Marion with a smile of hope on her face.

To think and talk about:
1 What do you think Marion has found?
2 What do you think Impossible Powder is?
   What might be the effects of Never Known To Fail Magic Mixture, Surprise Syrup or Demon Dust?
3 Do you think it would be wise to try some of these things?
4 Is there anything else you think Marion should examine?
5 What do you think she will do next?

2.3e Group prediction — 2 AT1/3c; AT2/3c-e
© Collins Educational 1990.

Name_____

Mrs. Canby's Cottage
(Part 3)

Dust swirled all around Marion as she lifted the witch's ancient spell book off the shelf. She carried it over to the table by the window and opened it at the contents page.

'How to change yourself (or anyone else) into all sorts of interesting things,' it read. 'Big things, page one; Small Things, page 7; Horrible Things, page 12, etc.'

Marion began to think. Suppose she were to change herself into something small enough to escape under the door. Then she would be free, but very small. If she were to come back to drink a Grow-Bigger potion she would be too big to get out again.

If she were to change herself into something big in the first place, she might be able to smash down the door, but then she would be too big to get out. She could of course drink a Grow-Smaller potion, but what if she grew too small? How much or how little of anything would she need to drink?

'This is not as easy as it seems,' she said to herself. She sat down in the armchair to think.

To talk and think about:
1 Were you right in guessing what Marion had found?
2 Do you think she would be wise to use the spellbook? Why?
3 How would you use it if you were Marion?
4 Think of as many ways as possible in which the story might end.

Mrs. Canby's Cottage
(Part 4)

As Marion sank into the armchair there was a mysterious creaking sound and the cupboard door opened. She sat up in astonishment. Through the door she could see a path leading into the wood. Without a moment's hesitation she was out of the chair and racing through the door. It slammed shut just too late to stop her.

The branches of the trees overhanging the path reached down to clutch at her hair, and thorns plucked at the hem of her dress, but Marion ran on. Then without warning the path opened into a sunlit clearing. A pretty cottage stood there, woodsmoke curling from its chimney.

Marion ran to the door, and rapped the shiny brass knocker. As the door opened she collapsed into the arms of a kind old lady.

The next thing she remembered was waking in a bright and cheerful bedroom. A doctor was sitting at her bedside and the kind old lady was speaking to him.

'Just think, Doctor Young,' she was saying, 'Marion came to look after me in my convalescence, and now I'm looking after her.'

'It's strange how things turn out, Mrs. Canby,' the doctor smiled. 'She must have got lost in the woods, and thought the witch's cottage was yours.'

'But she's quite safe now,' said Mrs. Canby.

'Yes,' said Marion, 'I'm quite safe now. Thanks to you.'

To think and talk about:
1 Is this how you thought the story would end?
2 How would you have ended the story?
3 Did you guess that Marion had gone to the wrong cottage?
   Read the story again. What clues are there that might have told you?
4 What might Marion have learned from her experience?
5 Think of a better title for the story.

2.3g Group prediction — 4
© Collins Educational 1990. AT1/3c; AT2/3c-e

Unit 4

Title — Games
Theme — Games
Stimuli — from *The Hermit and the Bear*
by John Yeoman, Andre Deutsch

AT1 Speaking/listening

3a	prediction
3i	explaining how and why things happen
3a	projection — reflecting on own feelings
3c	reasoning
3c-d	conducting a poll about the games children play
3c-d	finding out if boys spend more time playing then girls do

ATs 1-4 Word skills

- verbs — replacing "got" and "get" with a better verb
- crossword

AT2 Reading

3b; d	cloze procedure
3b-d	literal/inferential/reading for the main idea
3b-d	reading for detail
3d	using detailed information to match games to children
3f	skimming

AT3 Writing

3a	joining sentences — using "and" or "but" — without using "and"
3d	explaining the rules of "Snap"

Cloze passage:

The actual words used by the author in this extract are included here for reference purposes only. They should not be regarded as the correct answers — 1) and 2) arranged 3) pile 4) crumpled 5) after 6) isn't 7) we 8) end.

Activity sheets:

2.4a board game — developing from basic rules **AT1/3c-e; AT2/3f; AT3/3a & d**

2.4b fact sheet — sports **AT2/3f, AT3/3d**

Notes:

2.4a Checkpoint board game

This sheet provides a board for a car rally game called *Checkpoint* which the children can develop for themselves. They will need to prepare hazard cards, and general knowledge questions and answers.

Rules:

1 Each player has a counter and moves along the road according to throws of the dice.

2 If a player lands on a *Hazard* square he must draw a *Hazard* card.

3 If during a move a player lands on or passes over a *Checkpoint* square, he must stop on that square and a friend draws a *Checkpoint* card. If he answers that question wrongly he misses a turn.

4 The winner is the first past the chequered flag.

The children will first need to discuss the type of hazards they may meet on a car rally e.g. skidding off the road, getting stuck in mud, engine failure, taking a wrong turn etc. They will then have to decide the penalties appropriate to each hazard e.g. miss 1 or more turns, throw a six to move on etc. The checkpoint cards are the quiz element in the game. The children will decide on the questions. They may be general knowledge throughout, or divided into specialist categories. Each checkpoint may then have a particular category of questions or the children may choose for themselves. Alternatively, a throw of the dice may decide the type of question. The questions are to be devised by the children. Each question must be accompanied by an answer, any disputes to be settled by reference books or the teacher.

The *Hazard* and *Checkpoint* cards are then made and placed in two piles at the side of the board, and the game is ready to begin.

Listening skills: AT1/3d; AT2/3f; AT3/3c-d
2.4c handling aural information — listening for detail/adding detail to a map Side 1, track 3 Tape Counter _____

This track features two members of the Dawson Gang who plan to hold up the Wells Fargo stage-coach. The children are asked to mark places and routes on the map as the plans are discussed. (Please see the answer cards in the Appendices for the correct map details.)

Follow-up activities on this sheet include using reference books, speculation, writing a story about the robbery, and an imagined description of a ghost town at dusk.

2.4d handling aural information — following instructions/recording observations/speculation

Side 1, track 4   Tape Counter _____

The children are asked to use the instructions on the tape to make a paper helicopter. They then conduct simple experiments, record their observations and speculate on the results. They will need a pair of scissors and a paper clip. **AT1/3d; AT3/3d**

Speaking and listening:

1 After the children have developed and played the *Checkpoint* game, talk about a game called 'Wells Fargo' based on the listening skills sheet **2.4c**. Devise a board, objectives, rules, cards etc. Use the map on **2.4c** as a guide to board layout. **AT1/3a, c & d**

2 Discuss the function of rules in games. What would happen if there were no set rules? How important is a referee? How many times have the children's games come to a halt for lack of clear rules or a referee? What did they do about it? **AT1/3c**

3 Ask the children to talk to their grandparents about games they played as children. Wherever possible try to get tape-recordings of these reminiscences. Such tapes would be a valuable classroom resource. Discuss any of these games which are new to the children. Ask them to write out the rules and then to play them. Draw pictures or take photographs as they are played and make a class book of 'Children's Games'.

   Make a list of those games which were played by grandparents and are still popular with children today. **AT1/3c; AT3/3b**

4 If there are children or teachers of other cultural backgrounds, in the school, ask them about their games. Write the rules and play them. **AT1/3c; AT3/3b**

5 Collect skipping rhymes and others used in children's games. Listen to their rhymes and discuss their importance to the games. Record these rhymes. Make an illustrated book of them for the reference library. **AT1/3c; AT3/3b**

6 Use skipping and playground rhymes in choral speech. These can provide the links to poems about the playground and children's games. **AT1/3c & d**

7 Use a portable tape-recorder to record a commentary on the next match played by your school. Interview members of the two teams both before and after the match. Use the recording to write up an account of the match. **AT1/3c, d & a**

8 Action Word Sentences: One child supplies a verb and another has to make up a sentence containing that verb. **AT1/3c & d**

9 Group story: One child (or the teacher) begins a story by making up the first sentence. Each child in turn adds a sentence until the story is finished. A tape-recording of this will provide material for discussion of other possible lines of story development. **AT1/3c & d.**

Follow-up activities:

1 Make lists of different categories of games: indoor and outdoor, seasonal, boys' and girls' games, etc. **AT3/3d**

2 Write poems about games. The outline idea on activity sheet **2.3a** could be adapted to such poems. Instead of adjectives, verbs could be brainstormed for a number of sports, and verses built up using them. **AT3/3d; ATs 1-4**

3 Collect everyday expressions about games and playing. Illustrate and display them. Here is a selection.

   All work and no play makes Jack a dull boy.
   A miss is as good as a mile.
   When the cat's away the mice will play.
   To throw in the cards.
   To play fast and loose.
   Skating on thin ice.
   To play the game.
   Horse play.
   AT3/3d; ATs 1-4

4 Display a large map of the British Isles and mark on it the locations of famous sporting stadiums, football and cricket grounds, golf courses etc.

5 Collect the names of football teams. How many Uniteds are there? Or Cities, Wanderers etc? Which have other

names e.g. Gunners? Make a list of their grounds, colours, badges etc. **ATs 1-4; AT3/3d**

6 Look through the results of matches played by your school. Find what the average score per match has been this season. Compare it with previous seasons. Make a list of teams which have proved over a few seasons to be consistently better than the school team or consistently worse. Are there any teams against which you seem equally matched? **AT1/3d**; (Maths **AT1, 9 & 12**)

7 *Rhyming Snap*: Make cards of rhyming words and play Snap with them. Alternatively make cards of synonyms or antonyms. **AT3/3d**

8 *Happy Families*: Make cards of parents and young e.g. duck, drake, duckling. **AT3/3d**

9 Brainstorm words to build up a crossword like the one in Unit 4. The children could then invent their own clues. **AT3/3d**

10 Make a list of places such as school, the park, the beach, the shops etc. Then brainstorm appropriate verbs for each location. **AT3/3d**

Checkpoint

Discuss with your teacher how to make this an exciting car rally game.

H = Hazard square
C = Checkpoint

2.4a Board game
© Collins Educational 1990. AT1/3c-d; AT2/3f; AT3/3a & d

Sports Fact Sheet

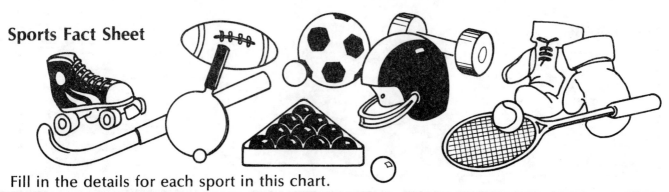

Fill in the details for each sport in this chart.

Sport	No. of players per side	Official	Score	Special clothing/equipment
Football	11	Referee	Goals	shirt, shorts, boots, ball
Netball				
Hockey				
Cricket				
Tennis				
Snooker				
Rugby Union				
Rugby League				
Rounders				
American Football				
Ice Hockey				
Baseball				
Basketball				
Volley Ball				
Golf				
Boxing				

On a separate sheet of paper write an account of any match you have seen or taken part in. Make your account as exciting as you can.

2.4b Fact sheet — sports
© Collins Educational 1990. AT2/3f; AT3/3d

The Hold-Up

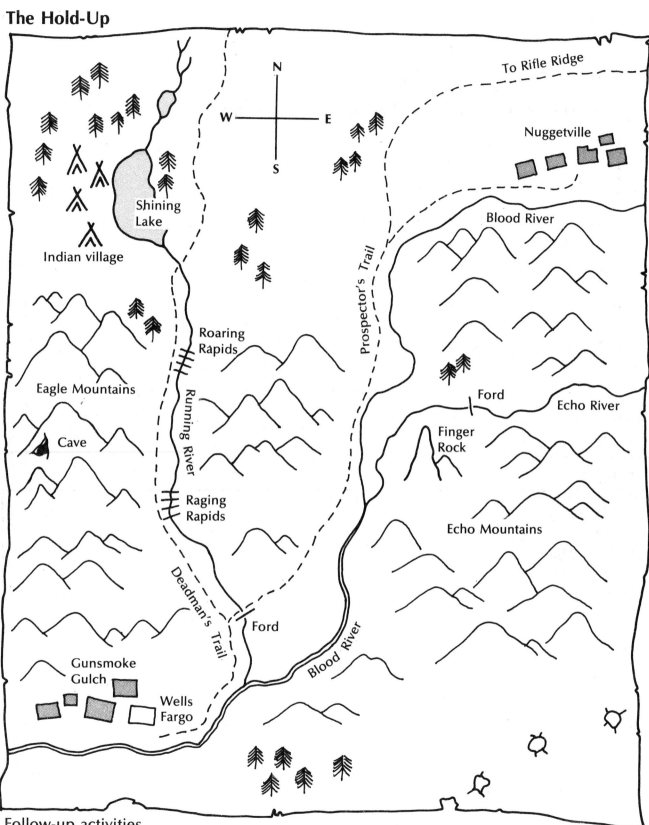

Follow-up activities

1 Nuggetville is now a ghost town. Find out what a ghost town is. Why do you think it is called Nuggetville? The name Prospector's Trail should give you a clue.

2 Write the story of the hold-up. Perhaps it does not go according to plan. Use the map to help you with your story.

3 Imagine you ride into a ghost town at dusk. Describe what you see and hear, and how you feel as the sun sets and shadows fall.

2.4c Handling aural information
© Collins Educational 1990. AT1/3d; AT2/3f; AT3/3c-d

Name_____

ENGLISH
ALIVE

Level 2
Master

2.4d

Helicopters

Listen to the tape. Then follow the instructions in the box.

> *Things to do with your helicopter.*
> 1   Drop your helicopter to the floor. What happens?
>
> _____
>
> _____
>
> 2   Cut out and make the second helicopter. Drop both helicopters together. What do you notice?
>
> _____
>
> _____
>
> 3   Why do you think this is?
>
> _____
>
> _____

Unit 5

Title — Festivals of Light
Theme — Festivals of Light
Stimuli — Factual passage and photographs.
'A Birthday Poem' by James Simmons from *The Selected James Simmons* (Blackstaff Press).
'My Party' by Kit Wright, from *Rabitting On* (Collins).

AT1 Speaking/listening
3a & c discussing festivals of light

ATs 1-4 Word skills
● opposites
● making adjectives from nouns

AT2 Reading
3b; d context clues
3b-d finding facts
3d appreciation of verse
3d inference
3f sorting into alphabetical lists
3f using reference books to learn more about festivals

AT3 Writing
3a paragraph building — completing a sentence and adding a second sentence
3a-b joining sentences with because
3d letter writing — a reply to an invitation
3b-c & e description of a party

AT4 Spelling
3a homonyms

Activity sheets:
2.5a homonyms **AT2/3f; ATs 1-4**
2.5b joining sentences with because (Skillmaster) **AT3/3a**
2.5c context clues (Skillmaster) **AT2/3d**
2.5d recipe — Pepparkakor Biscuits (St. Lucia Biscuits) **AT2/3f**
2.5e rangoli patterns **ATs 1-4**

Speaking and listening
1 Talk about the use of light as
   i) a symbol of hope e.g. a light in a window, lighthouse etc.
   ii) a religious symbol e.g. Jesus is the Light of the World. **AT1/3c**

2 Compare the different festivals of light and look into the beliefs and stories that surround them. The following notes give some background information.

Notes on the Festivals of Light featured in Unit 5
1 *Divali* (often Diwali of Dipavali)
Divali is celebrated by Hindus and Sikhs. It takes place around the end of October and is named after the divas (small clay lamps) which are lit in windows to invite Laxmi (Lakshmi) the goddess of wealth to bless the house. It is a happy festival, in many respects similar to our Christmas, and involves the sending of Divali cards and the exchange of presents.

There are many legends traditionally associated with Divali, but the most famous is the story of Rama and Sita.

Rama and *Sita*
Rama was the son of a wise king and should have succeeded him to the throne. His stepmother, however, persuaded the king to send Rama and his wife Sita into exile with his brother Lakshmana. During this exile they faced many problems, the main one being the capture of Sita by the ten-headed demon king, Ravana, who took her away to his island kingdom. After a desperate search for his wife, Rama was helped by Hanuman, the monkey warrior. All the animals joined together to build a bridge from India to the island. After Rama had crossed the bridge a terrible battle took place in which Rama killed the demon king with a special bow given him by Dirga, goddess of motherhood. Rama then rescued Sita and they returned triumphantly to Ayodhya where he was made king.

It is said that the whole city was lit up to guide the couple home. The shining lights stood for the triumph of good over evil, and were an invitation to Lakshmi, goddess of wealth, to bestow good fortune on the people of Ayodhya, as she had on its true King and Queen.

The Sikhs also celebrate Divali. Their religion was founded about five hundred years ago by Guru Nanak. He was followed by nine more Gurus (or teachers). The last Guru apoointed the

Sikh's holy book to be the next Guru and from then on this holy book became Guru Granth Sahib.

The sixth Guru, Guru Har Gabind (1595-1644), was a great military leader as well as a religious leader. He was imprisoned by the Mughal Emperor, Jehangir, and eventually released around the time of Divali making it a time of great celebration for Sikhs too. The temples (Guruwara) are all lighted with little lights, as is the beautiful Golden Temple at Amritsar, in memory of the release of their spiritual leader.

2   *Advent*
This is celebrated by Christians all around the world. Advent is the four weeks leading up to Christmas and means 'coming'. It is the time of year when Christians get ready for the birth of Jesus. Usually advent calendars count down the days to Christmas, but all over Europe Advent Wreaths or crowns are made with candles to mark the passing of these four weeks.

An Advent Crown
To make a simple Advent Crown you will need:
  2 potatoes
  4 candles
  red or silver foil
  sprigs of holly
  mistletoe
  flameproof tinsel

1) Cut each potato in half and use a potato peeler or apple corer to make a hole in the rounded end of each potato for the candle to sit securely.
2) Cover the potato halves in foil and stand each piece firmly on a plate or aluminium tray.
3) Arrange sprigs of holly etc. around the four potato halves, pushing the stems in so that they keep fresh.
4) Wind tinsel in and out of the greenery, filling in any gaps.
5) Put the four candles into the 'holders' and the wreath or crown is ready.
6) Light the first candle on the first Sunday in Advent, two candles on the following Sunday etc.

3   *Hannukah* (Chanukah)
Hannukah is a Jewish festival which takes place in December. The story of Hannukah tells how a Syrian leader, Antiochus, invaded Israel and captured the holy city of Jerusalem. Antiochus then invaded the Temple and desecrated it by killing a pig on the altar. The Jews rose up in revolt and, led by a young man called Judas the Maccabee, they began a three year battle. Eventually Judas and his army recaptured the Holy City. They entered the Temple, threw out all the Greek idols and began to clean it out. They searched for holy oil to relight the Temple lamp which was to be kept burning continually before the altar. They found only one small pot, but its oil kept the lamp burning miraculously for eight days, giving them time to prepare more.

The festival of Hannukah lasts for eight days and celebrates the reclamation of their holy temple. The Menorah, the special candlestick used in this festival, reminds Jews of the miracle of the small pot of oil. One candle is lit for each day of the festival and after being lit it must burn for at least half an hour. No one is allowed to work by its light. Hannukah is a time of great happiness and the menorah are put in windows to show the outside world the joy that is felt inside.

4   *The Feast of St. Lucia* (St. Lucy)
This festival takes place in Sweden on December 13th, the shortest day of the year.

St. Lucia was a Christian martyr who was executed in AD 304, having refused to renounce her faith. Legends say that St. Lucia took food to Christians who were hiding from the Romans in caves underneath Rome. To keep her hands free for carrying the food she wore candles in a crown on her head.

In the Feast of St. Lucia one of the daughters of the family gets up very early and dresses in a white gown and red sash. She then puts on a crown of green leaves and white candles, and takes coffee and special biscuits to the rest of her family who are still in bed. Towns and villages have their own 'official' St. Lucia and the day is spend in parades, music and dancing.

A recipe for the special Pepparkakor biscuits has been included on Activity Master **2.5d**.

5   Other festivals of light include Christingle, the birthday of Buddah and Bonfire Night.

Follow-up activities:

1   Make a collection of words that have two or more different meanings. Use a display board and ask the children to illustrate the different meanings by means of little sketches. **AT3/3d**

2   Make a display of birthday cards, party invitations, hats, whistles etc. Ask the children to donate these wherever possible.

3   Have the children design their own party invitations and birthday cards. **AT3/3d**

4   Collect and display festival cards: Christmas, Divali, Hannukah etc.

5   Make the Pepparkakor biscuits (**2.5d**) and celebrate the feast of St. Lucia in your school. Choose a girl to dress up in the traditional way and distribute freshly baked biscuits around the school.   **AT2/3f, AT1/3d**

6   Make some little 'diva' lamps out of clay and place a nite-lite candle inside. Traditionally these are placed in the windows.

7   Another activity for Divali is to make Rangoli patterns. These are decorative shapes with circles, flowers, leaves and other patterns that are drawn on the floor and coloured in with chalks, coloured flour and spices. Simpler versions can be made using coloured chalks or powder paint on black sugar paper. Some rangoli patterns have been included on Activity Master **2.5e**. These are for colouring in, but are equally useful as stimuli for larger versions of rangoli patterns.

8   Drama: Act out the Ramayana (story of Rama and Sita), making monkey masks and dressing many children as the different animals that built the legendary bridge from India to Sri Lanka.   **AT1/3a & d**

9   Many of these ideas are suitable for use in a class assembly, concert or a festival of light.   **AT1/3a-d**

10   Observation: Light a candle and watch it flicker. Brainstorm to describe words that the children see. Make a display of these words in candle outlines. This makes a valuable resource for poetry and story writing.   **AT3/3d**

11   Science experiments: Use a prism to show the refraction of light into rainbow colours. (Science **AT15/3**)
   Use a candle in a jar to show the need for oxygen.   (Science **AT9/3b**)

12   Make candles using a cold wax and string kit. These can then be carved with a cocktail stick and given as presents.

13   Make an Advent candle by dividing a long candle into twenty five segments. The numbers can be scratched on with a cocktail stick. Each day light the candle until it has burned down to the next mark.

14   Stories and poems: **AT2/3a**
   The Eight Lights of Hannukkiya, retold by Leo Paulac (Orbis Beehive)
   The Owl Who Was Afraid of the Dark, Jill Tomlinson (Young Puffin)
   Seasons of Splendour, Madhur Jaffrey (Pavillion Books)
   'The Christmas Party', Adeline White, *Book of a Thousand Poems* (Evans).

Acknowledgements:
The following books have been useful to the authors in developing this unit:
Festival: Divali, Olivia Bennett (Macmillan Educational)
Festival: Divali (Teacher's Notes), Rosalind Kerven (Macmillan Educational)
Exploring Religion: Festivals, Olivia Bennett (Bell & Hyman)
Light, P. & V. Smeltzer (Lion)
I am a Sikh (Franklin Watts)
I am a Jew (Franklin Watts)
The Lion Christmas Book, compiled by Mary Batchelor.

Words With Different Meanings

Sometimes a word can have two meanings:

> Ice is very <u>cold</u>.
> Jenny had a <u>cold</u>.

In the first sentence <u>cold</u> is opposite to <u>hot</u>.
In the second sentence a <u>cold</u> is a kind of <u>illness</u>.

Write what the underlined word means in each of these sentences.
Use a dictionary to help you.

1 I like to <u>roll</u> down the hill. _____

2 In the cafe Pat had soup and a bread <u>roll</u>. _____

3 My grandma lives in a <u>flat</u>. _____

4 The floor was smooth and <u>flat</u>. _____

5 Billy wore a black <u>tie</u> with his white shirt. _____

6 My sister can't even <u>tie</u> her shoe-laces yet. _____

7 The window was stuck <u>fast</u>. _____

8 Dad's new car is very <u>fast</u>. _____

Use these words in sentences of your own to show two different meanings.

1 *catch*   a) _____

            b) _____

2 *lie*   a) _____

            b) _____

3 *fly*   a) _____

            b) _____

2.5a Skillmaster — homonyms
© Collins Educational 1990. ATs 1-4

Name_____

Making Sentences Using 'because'

Read this sentence: | The cake tasted horrible. |

Why did it taste horrible? We can say:

| The cake tasted horrible *because it was burnt.* |

or | The cake tasted horrible *because mother forgot to add sugar.* |

We use *because* to tell why the cake tasted horrible.

Match each beginning with its correct ending.

1 The girl felt dizzy - - - - - - - - - - - - - because they had had an argument.
2 John and Karl were not speaking   because he had found his bone.
3 Spot wagged his tail   because she had been doing cartwheels.
4 The window was broken   because there was a hole in the bottom.
5 Jane was laughing   because the ball had gone through it.
6 The ship sank quickly   because the clown was so funny.

Finish these sentences.
1 Pamela and Judith were friends because _____

_____

2 I don't like beefburgers because _____

_____

3 The clock had stopped because _____

_____

4 Mum could not find her purse because _____

_____

5 They all sang beautifully because _____

_____

6 The witch laughed wickedly because _____

_____

7 I knew we would win at football because _____

_____

8 The rocket slowed down because _____

_____

2.5b Skillmaster — joining sentences with *because*
© Collins Educational 1990. AT3/3a

Reading Clues

Sometimes when we read there are words we don't know or don't understand. Yet if we read carefully we often find clues to help us.

Do you know what transparent means?

Read this sentence carefully. | Glass is good for windows because it is <u>transparent</u>. |

Does transparent mean   a)   *see through*

b)   *made of metal?*   Transparent means *see through*.

Read these sentences carefully and underline the correct meaning.

1   We went out of the house and sat on the <u>verandah</u>.
   a)   a porch joined onto a house   b)   road

2   The <u>climate</u> in the Sahara desert is different to ours. It hardly ever rains.
   a)   language   b)   weather

3   The Spanish <u>galleon</u> sailed forward with all her guns firing.
   a)   soldier   b)   old sailing ship

4   Janice's grandma picked the big purple <u>rhododendron</u> and smelt it.
   a)   a flowering plant   b)   a piece of cloth

5   The servant went into the <u>larder</u> to fill a tray full of food.
   a)   a room where food is kept   b)   a shop

6   The woman who rescued the little boy was called a <u>heroine</u>.
   a)   nurse   b)   woman who does something brave

7   The man was very <u>anxious</u> about his injured wife.
   a)   pleased   b)   worried

8   The builder spread the <u>mortar</u> and then laid the bricks.
   a)   a mixture used to make bricks stick together   b)   soil

2.5c   Skillmaster — context clues
© Collins Educational 1990. AT2/3d

Name_____

Pepparkakor Biscuits
(St. Lucia Biscuits)

What you will need:

400g	plain flour
1 tspn	bicarbonate of soda
1½ tspn	ground ginger and cinnamon
230g	margarine
230g	dark brown sugar
2	egg whites

Method:

1 Sift flour, bicarbonate of soda, the cinnamon and ginger and place on one side.

2 In a bowl, cream the butter and the sugar until fluffy. Add the egg whites and beat until well mixed.

3 Gradually add the dry ingredients until it forms a dough. Leave in a cool place for 5-10 minutes.

4 Heat oven to 350°C (Gas mark 4) and lightly grease a baking sheet.

5 Roll out the dough to about ½cm thick. Cut into fancy shapes (traditionally stars and rings) and place these, well spaced, on the baking sheet.

6 Place in the centre of the oven for 10-12 minutes until light brown round the edge.

7 Allow to cool on a wire rack. Store in an airtight container.

8 These biscuits can also be decorated with icing and cherries or even melted chocolate.

2.5d Recipe
© Collins Educational 1990. AT2/3f

Name_____

Rangoli Patterns

Unit 6

Title — Time
Theme — Time
Stimuli — 'Time Trouble' by Penelope Lively, from *Uninvited Ghosts*, Heinemann.

AT1 Speaking/listening
3a	creating and developing an imaginary situation
3a-c	reporting on past experiences

ATs 1-4 Word skills
- everyday expressions about time
- similes
- verbs — past tense
- parts in a whole — finding short words in longer ones

AT2 Reading
3b-c	checking facts
3b; d	cloze procedure
3d-e	prediction
3d	inferences
3d-f	sequencing — completing a time line (from passage)
3f	calendar
3f	using a dictionary

AT3 Writing
3a	paragraph building — writing a middle sentence
3b	joining sentences with 'who' or 'whom'
3b-c & e	imaginative story
3d	thank you letter for a present

Cloze passage:
The actual words used by the author are given here for reference only. They should not be regarded as the correct answers — 1) in 2) with 3) about 4) what 5) loud 6) mood 7) then 8) had 9) into 10) late.

Activity sheets:
2.6a verbs — past tense (Skillmaster) **ATs 1-4**
2.6b joining sentences with *who* or *which* (Skillmaster) **ATs 1-4; AT3/3a**
2.6c T.V. programme schedules **AT2/3d & f**
2.6d writing — imaginative stories **AT3/3b-c**
2.6e group prediction *The Door in the Wall* — 1 **AT1/3c; AT2/3c-e**
2.6f group prediction *The Door in the Wall* — 2 **AT1/3c; AT2/3c-e**
2.6g group prediction *The Door in the Wall* — 3 **AT1/3c; AT2/3c-e**
2.6h group prediction *The Door in the Wall* — 4 **AT1/3c; AT2/3c-e**

Notes:
2.6d Before using this sheet, brainstorm ideas about time machines.

Speaking and listening:
1 Read *The Door in the Wall* group prediction story **2.6e-f**. Discuss possible story developments and endings. **AT2/3a & c; AT1/3c & d**

2 Discuss these proverbs connected with time: **AT1/3d**
   Any time means no time
   Better late than never
   First come, first served
   A stitch in time saves nine
   Early to bed, early to rise . . .

3 Discuss common similes. **AT1/3d**

4 Yesterday and Today: One child gives a sentence with a verb in the present tense. He then challenges another child to begin a sentence with 'Yesterday . . .', and to change the tense of his verb.
   The game can be made more competitive if it is played as a team game with scores. **AT1/3d; AT1/3a**

5 Talk about time capsules. What objects would the children put into a time capsule to show future generations what life is like today? Obvious items are newspapers and photographs, but what other things would be interesting and informative to future generations? **AT1/3d**
   Make a list of items for a time capsule. What would such a capsule be made of? Where should it be buried? **AT3/3c & d**
   Make a time capsule, fill it and bury it in the school grounds. Decide on a date to dig it up again.

6 Discuss ideas for an audio or video tape about your school, as if for a time capsule. This would require an introduction, a commentary, sound pictures of different parts of the building and grounds, interviews with children and staff, songs, poems etc. etc. When all has been carefully planned, record the tape. **AT1/3d**

Follow-up activities:

1 Ask the children to keep a detailed diary for a week so that it can be included in the time capsule (see note 5 above). Write descriptions of the school and the staff. Ask each child to make a list about his favourite things eg books, food, T.V. programmes, records and pop stars, sportsmen etc. Make predictions about what life will be like when the capsule is opened. **AT3/3b**

Place all these in the capsule and bury it in the school grounds. Dig it up before the children leave school. The children will then enjoy reading their own work and will be amused at how their ideas and feelings have changed in only a year or so.

2 Make a collection of different types of clocks:
Grandfather clock, cuckoo clock, candle clock, water clock, sundial, pocket watch, digital and analogue watches, alarm clock etc. Use pictures if actual clocks cannot be found.

3 Visit any local places which have animated clocks with figures moving when the clock strikes.

4 Ask the children to make as many words as they can using the letters of the words 'grandfather clock'. **ATs 1-4**

5 Construct a time machine in the corner of the classroom, using cardboard boxes and aluminium foil. Design a control panel for it. A roll of paper with dates going backwards and forwards at 50 or 100 year intervals could be used to set the machine for use. Alternatively four rolls with numbers from 0 to 9 could be used to set any date. An AD/BC setting could be incorporated.

Such a machine could then be a stimulus for a variety of work:
Story writing (see activity sheet **2.6c**), and poetry. **AT3/3b-c & d**
Transactional writing: instructions for using the machine, a log for recording its travels etc. **AT3/3d**
History: ask the children to select a date and then describe what they think life was like at that time. **AT1/3a-d**
Reference skills: use reference books to learn about different periods. **AT2/3f**
Drama: the children act out the building of the machine, travelling through time and the adventures they have in the past or future. Make and record suitable sound effects for the machine. **AT1/3a & d**

6 Make graphs of the children's favourite television programmes (Science **AT1/3f & g**). Bring in the schedules for the previous night's viewing. Ask the children to say which programmes they watched. Find out how many children watched each programme. Ask the children to work out how long they spent watching television that night. Find out if boys watch more television than girls do. (Maths **AT12/3a & b**)

Discuss the value of watching television. What other things might the children have done during that time?

7 Ask each child to make out a personal timetable for a typical day (Science **AT1/3i**). Compare this with others in the class and discuss similarities and differences. (English **AT2/3d; AT3/3d**)

8 Construct a pie chart showing how much time the children spend at school, sleeping, playing, etc. (Science **AT1/3f & g**; Maths **AT12/3a & b**)

9 Ask the children to imagine they are from the future and they come across the time capsule they buried (see previous notes). Write about this experience, and what future generations might think of our world. **AT3/3a-c**

10 Make water, sand, shadow and candle clocks. Can the children think of other ways of measuring time? Set them the problem of devising an original way to measure ten seconds, for example. Ask them to check their clocks with a stop watch. (Science **(AT16/3b)**

Name_____

Yesterday

Write these sentences as if they happened yesterday. Then colour the pictures.

I come home from school at half past three.

Yesterday I _____

Mum makes my tea at five o'clock.

Yesterday Mum _____

I do my homework at half past six.

Yesterday I _____

We watch television at half past eight.

Yesterday we _____

I eat my supper at nine o'clock.

Yesterday I _____

I go to bed at half past nine.

Yesterday I _____

2.6a Skillmaster — past tense
© Collins Educational 1990. ATs 1-4

Name_____

ENGLISH
ALIVE

Level 2
Master

2.6b

Joining Sentences

Look at these sentences.

> Peter is the boy. He won first prize in the poetry competition.

They can be joined by using **who.**

> Peter is the boy **who** won the poetry competition.

If we are talking about an **animal** or a **thing** we use **which** instead of who.

> Peter wrote a poem. The poem took first prize in the competition.
> Peter wrote a poem **which** took first prize in the competition.

Use **who** or **which** to join these sentences.

1   At the jumble sale Dad bought a clock. The clock would not work.

_____

2   Last week I met a man. The man knew my grandad.

_____

3   My uncle owned a dog. His dog chased the postman down the street.

_____

4   Yesterday my sister found a book. It was over a hundred years old.

_____

5   The policeman stopped the driver. The driver was speeding.

_____

6   I spoke to a man. He told me where the Post Office was.

_____

7   He saw a girl. She was crying.

_____

8   He bought some flowers. They cost him a lot of money.

_____

Write two sentences of your own, using **who.**

_____

_____

Write two sentences of your own, using **which.**

_____

_____

2.6b Skillmaster — joining sentences with *who* or *which*
© Collins Educational 1990. ATs 1-4; AT3/3a

Television Programmes

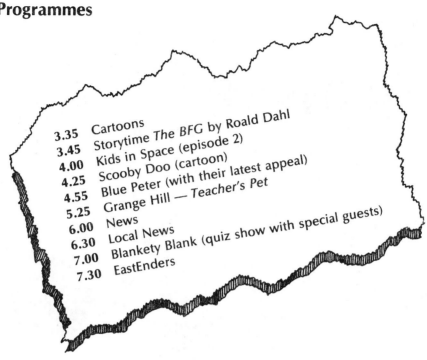

3.35 Cartoons
3.45 Storytime *The BFG* by Roald Dahl
4.00 Kids in Space (episode 2)
4.25 Scooby Doo (cartoon)
4.55 Blue Peter (with their latest appeal)
5.25 Grange Hill — *Teacher's Pet*
6.00 News
6.30 Local News
7.00 Blankety Blank (quiz show with special guests)
7.30 EastEnders

Look at the T.V. timetable and answer these questions.

1 At what time does the News start? _____

2 At what time do the first cartoons end? _____

3 What could you watch after Blue Peter? _____
4 What programmes would be on if you switched on at:

   3.45 _____   7.00 _____

   5.35 _____   4.15 _____?

5 What kind of programme is Blankety Blank? _____

   _____

6 How many cartoons can you watch? _____

7 What will Blue Peter tell you about today? _____

8 For how long could you watch news programmes? _____

9 What is tonight's episode of Grange Hill called? _____

10 How do you know 'Kids in Space' is a recent programme? _____

   _____

2.6c TV Programme schedules
© Collins Educational 1990. AT2/3d & f

Name_____

The Time Machine

_____
_____
_____
_____
_____
_____
_____
_____
_____
_____
_____

2.6d Writing — imaginative story
© Collins Educational 1990. AT3/3b–c

The Door in the Wall: Part 1

The three children were dressed all in blue, and hoods hid their faces. Jamal began to watch them. Something about them made him curious. They were walking close together and as Jamal moved to see round their hoods they turned their heads, hiding their faces from him.

He crossed the street and followed them into Acacia Avenue, slowing his pace to match their strange, shuffling walk. On one side of the street was a high brick wall. The hooded children stopped there and knocked three times at a red door which Jamal could not remember having seen before.

He was just considering this fact when the door opened and the children passed through. Jamal hurried forward, but the door slammed firmly shut before he could reach it. There was no knob or handle of any kind. There was, however, a kind of window with a sliding wooden shutter across it. Jamal was filled with curiosity. Who were the children and what was behind the door in the wall?

He gave three sharp raps on the door, just as the children had done. For a few seconds nothing happened. Then the wooden window slid back and two green eyes peered out at him. They blinked twice and then the window slid shut again. Jamal waited for the door to open, but nothing happened. He knocked again, but the door remained firmly closed.

'Now what?' he thought.

To think and talk about:
1   Who do you think the children are?
    Why do you think they hid their faces from Jamal?
2   What do you think is behind the wall?
3   Why do you think Jamal had never seen the door before?
4   Do you think that Jamal will get inside the door?
    What do you think he will do next?

2.6e Group prediction — 1
© Collins Educational 1990. AT1/3c; AT2/3c-e

Name_____

ENGLISH
ALIVE

Level 2
Master

2.6f

The Door in the Wall: Part 2

Jamal hurried home. He opened his wardrobe and picked out a selection of clothes. When he arrived back on Acacia Avenue he was dressed all in blue, the hood of his anorak hiding most of his face.

He shuffled up to the door and knocked three times, looking down at the pavement to hide his face. He heard the window open and slide shut again, but though he waited several minutes the door was not opened to him.

Jamal crossed the road and stood under a tree. He looked at the wall. It was far too high to see over or to climb. He was about to give up and go home when four more children rounded the corner and shuffled up to the red door. The leader rapped four times on the door and, quick as winking, the door opened and they passed through. Jamal raced across the street. He had a brief glimpse of trees before the door slammed shut.

He pulled his hood forward, knocked four times and waited. Nothing happened.

He went back to the tree across the road and wondered what to do. As he was thinking, a group of five children appeared shuffling towards the door. Jamal crossed the road and shuffled up behind them. They did not seem to notice him so he lowered his head to hide his face and stood at the back. One of the children knocked at the door. As the last of his five sharp raps sounded, the door opened and the children hurried forward with Jamal following them. All five children passed through, but the door slammed in Jamal's face. He beat on the door five times, but it remained closed.

Then, in a flash, he realised what he must do.

To think and talk about:
These are some of the ideas that passed through Jamal's head.

1 There is a garden behind the wall.
2 The children are all members of a secret club.
3 They are all going to some kind of meeting.
4 If I knew the secret of the club I could join them.
5 The number of knocks must be a kind of code.

Which of these do you agree with? What makes you think so?
If you think Jamal is right about a code, how do you think it works?
What do you think Jamal will do next?

2.6f Group prediction — 2
© Collins Educational 1990. AT2/3c-e

The Door in the Wall: Part 3

'Three children knocked three times, four children knocked four times and five children knocked five times.'

Jamal reached a decision. He set off across the road and once again stopped in front of the red door.

'There's only one of me,' he thought, 'so I will knock once!'

He knocked once and waited impatiently, but nothing happened. He was just about to give up completely when another thought occurred to him.

'Three, four, five . . . . . . SIX!'

Jamal knocked six times, and immediately the door was opened. His heart beating with excitement, Jamal passed through.

Trees grew all around him and paths led off in all directions. He followed one of them and soon he was at the edge of a beautiful garden with a fountain in the middle. All around him were little people in blue, but their hoods were down and Jamal could see that they were not children at all but gnomes. One of the gnomes approached him with a smile.

'Drink at the fountain and enjoy our garden,' he said with a friendly smile, 'but be sure to be out of here before four o'clock!'

Jamal cupped his hands and drank from the fountain. As he did so the gnomes came to him and shook his hand as if he were an old friend. For two hours he joined in all the games the gnomes played. He had never felt so happy.

Suddenly he heard a distant clock chiming four. He turned to run, but he was too late. The garden was empty of all his new friends. He hurried into the trees looking for the path to the red door, but in no time at all he was hopelessly lost.

Then just as he was beginning to think he would never get out a voice from out of the air spoke to him.

'Look under this tree. You will find three things. Two of them will help you find your way out. Choose carefully, and use them well.'

Jamal saw three things appear amongst the roots of the tree in front of him: a key, a bag of gold and a ball of wool.

'Now what shall I do? he said to himself.

To think and talk about:
1 Were you surprised to find the 'children' were gnomes? Say why.
2 Which objects do you think will help Jamal to get out?
3 How do you think he will use them?
4 Talk about the many different ways the story could end.
5 Which of these do you think is the most likely ending?

2.6g Group prediction — 3
© Collins Educational 1990. AT1/3c; AT2/3c-e

Name_____

ENGLISH
ALIVE

Level 2
Master

2.6h

The Door in the Wall: Part 4

After some thought Jamal picked up the key. He guessed this would open the red door. The ball of wool would help him too so he picked that up. Then he tried to pick up the bag of gold, but it was too heavy.

An idea came to him and he dropped the key. The bag of gold was now easy to lift. He stooped to pick up the key but was unable to do so. Reluctantly he dropped the gold and took the key.

He tied one end of the wool to the tree and set off along one of the many paths. The wool trailed behind him marking his route. That way he would not find himself walking round in circles.

Slowly the ball of wool got smaller. As he got down to the last few metres he found the red door.

The key turned in the lock and the door opened. Jamal could see Acacia Avenue, but he turned round and headed back into the trees, following the trail of wool. Soon he was back at the tree and the bag of gold was where he had left it. Without the key he was able to pick up the gold. He set off at a run along the wool-marked path, clutching the bag of gold tightly to his chest.

The door was still ajar and with a shout of joy Jamal ran into Acacia Avenue. As he did so the bag of gold disappeared. He turned round in dismay to look for it, and noticed that the red door had disappeared too. Only a blank brick wall faced him.

Ever since that day Jamal has visited Acacia Avenue many times, but never again has he seen the red door or the blue gnomes.

To think and talk about
1   Do you think Jamal was right to have taken the gold?
     What would you have done?
2   Do you think it likely that he would have found the red door again if he had not
     taken the gold?
3   Say what you liked or didn't like about the story.
4   If you were the author what changes would you make?

2.6h Group prediction — 4
© Collins Educational 1990. AT1/3c; AT2/3c-e

Unit 7

Title — The Memory Tree
Theme — Memory
Stimuli — 'Clean Sheets' by Joan Aitken from *Tale of a One-Way Street*, (Jonathan Cape;
'The Camel' by Ogden Nash, included in *Versicles and Limericks* by Charles Connell (Beaver).

AT1 Speaking/listening
3a   recalling earliest memories

ATs 1-4 Word skills
●   pronouns

AT2 Reading
3b-e	literal/inferential/evaluative
3b; d	cloze procedure
3d	supplying missing instructions
3d	projection
3d-e	prediction
3f	recalling details of a picture
3f	flow diagram — planting a tree
3f	sequencing instructions
3f	memorising a poem
3f	using a dictionary

AT3 Writing
3a & d	flow chart
3b-c & e	imaginative writing, writer as participant
3b & e	personal experience

AT4 Spelling
3b   plurals: -ies and -s endings from -y words

Cloze passage:
The author's actual words are given here for reference only. They should not be regarded as the correct answers — 1) birthday 2) He 3) saddle 4) the 5) how 6) but 7) catch.

Activity sheets:
2.7a pronouns (Skillmaster) **ATs 1-4**
2.7b plurals: *-ies* and *-s* endings from *-y* words (Skillmaster) **AT4/3b**
2.7c story map — stimulus for imaginative story **AT3/3b-c**
2.7d Kim's Game **ATs 1-4**

Listening skills:
2.7e figure/ground differentiation — speaker in a noisy environment **AT1/3b**

Side 1, track 5   Tape counter _____
The children have to listen carefully to the words of a speaker in a noisy environment. They then have to pick the actual words spoken from a choice of four sentences. The correct answers are as follows:
1b) McKinlay has scored a goal for United!
2a) The train standing at platform 7 is running approximately ten minutes late.
3b) There's a gentleman to see you, Mr. Vines.
4c) The number 96 bus is always late.
5d) Let's go and get a drink.
6c) Get a move on. This tyre needs changing.

Speaking and listening:
1   Use sheet **2.7d** (Kim's Game). Get the children to study the sheet and then ask each other specific questions about it:
     e.g.   What was in the square next to the cotton reel?
           How many objects were in square C3?
           In which square was the drawing pin? etc. **AT1/3b & d**

2   Make a large Kim's Game grid on the classroom wall. Each time the children leave the room, remove or replace one of the items. See if the children can identify which one has been changed. **AT1/3d**

3   See if the children can remember the Ogden Nash verse they learned in Unit 7. **AT1/3b**

4   Give them other short poems and verses to learn in a similar way. **AT1/3b**

5   Use the writing the children have done about their earliest memories as a stimulus for a discussion of memory. What things can the children remember most vividly. Why do they think these memories are so vivid? **AT1/3c**

6   Get the children to ask the rest of their family about their earliest memories. If possible ask them to tape record these reminiscences for the class to listen to. **AT1/3b & c**

Drama: The children sit in a circle. Someone starts making up and telling a story. After a while he stops and the person on his left continues it. This requires the children to remember what has gone on before in order to develop the story. When the story has been completed, the children act it out **AT1/3c & d**

8 *Drama:* (As stimulus or follow-up work to sheet **2.7c**, the Story Map). Place large sheets of paper on the floor as a pathway. Each child selects a sheet and then draws on it a place or an event. A quick sketch will suffice, but a more careful picture can be drawn later to form an attractive classroom display.

   When the drawings are complete, the children work in groups along the road and act out the adventures they have on their journey.

   The road can be rearranged so that no two journeys are ever alike. **AT1/3c & d**

9 Play memory games such as 'I went to the market . . .', and Kim's Game, using objects on a tray. See *Level 1 Teacher's Resource Book* for further ideas. **AT1/3c & d**

Follow-up activities

1 Construct a time-line on the wall of the classroom and plot the dates and events that are the children's earliest memories.

2 Set up a 'Memory Lane' in the corner of the classroom, with old school photographs, programmes from school productions etc., and photographs of the children when they were younger. Newspaper cuttings can also be included. The contributions to this display should come from the children. They should represent the children's memories. **AT1/3a; AT3/3d**

3 *Look and Draw:* Draw a large shape or simple picture on the board. Ask the children to study it for a few moments and then cover it. The children have to draw the shape from memory. This can then be made increasingly difficult by making the drawing more complex and/or the time allowed shorter.

4 *Listen and Draw:* This is an aural alternative to Look and Draw. Here a description is given to the children and they draw the picture from memory. The level of difficulty can be increased by making the description longer or more complex. **AT1/3d**

5 Ask the children to make lists of instructions for everyday activities such as getting ready for P.E., changing a library book etc. Emphasis should be placed on logical sequence and small stages of instruction. **AT3/3d; AT1/3a**

6 Make flow charts of existing sets of instructions e.g. fire drill, instructions for playing board games etc. **AT3/3d**

Computer program listing:

Memory Game

This program presents the children with a sequence of five colours to be memorised.

It has been written for the BBC range of computers, but can be modified to run on other machines.

Please note:
This program is longer and more complex than the earlier listings and consequently more prone to keying in errors. If the program does not run correctly please check the listing carefully.

The program is very simple and capable of considerable improvement. The user is invited to ake any modifications he wishes.

To reduce or increase the time each colour is displayed change the '2000' in line 110. '1000' will half the time, whilst '4000' will double it.

Lines 2-6 may be omitted. The program runs as follows:

The program	*Line nos.*
Arrays are set up for the random colours and also for the children's answers.	10-20
Mode 7 is selected and the wrong answers score is set to zero.	30-40
The procedure PROCdice is called to select random colours.	50
The screen is set up and instructions given.	60-80
This is done mainly by PROCintro.	280-340
the computer then displays the colours selected.	90-120
The children are then asked "Which order?" and "Key in only the FIRST letter of each colour."	130-150
PROCinput asks for the order of the colours.	350-370
calls, PROCcheck to see if this is correct,	450-520
and then gives the children a	390-440

score.
The program then re-runs itself. 180

```
  2   REM MEMORY GAME
  6   REM B.SCHOLES 1988
 10   DIM N(5)
 20   DIM A$(5)
 30   MODE 7
 40   WRONG=0
 50   PROCdice
 60   PRINTTAB(2,2)CHR$(129);"Red
      ";CHR$130;"Green ";CHR$131;
      "Yellow ";CHR$132; "Blue ";CHR$133;
      "Purple"
 70   PROCintro
 80   VDU28,12,18,25,4
 90   FOR T=1 TO 5
100   FOR Y=1TO8:
      PRINTTAB(0,Y)CHR$(128+N(T)):
      CHR$157:SPC(11):CHR$156;:NEXT Y
110   FOR wait=1TO2000: NEXTwait
120   NEXT T
130   CLS:VDU26:PRINTTAB(11,6)"Which
      order?"
140   PRINT' "Key in only the FIRST letter
      of each"
150   PRINT"colour."
160   T=0
170   PROCinput
180   A=GET:RUN
190   DEF PROCdice
200   N(1)=RND(5)
210   REPEAT
220   N(2)=RND(5)
230   UNTIL N(2)<>N(1)
240   REPEAT: N(3)=RND(5):UNTIL
      N(3)<>N(1) AND N(3)<>N(2)
250   REPEAT:N(4)=RND(5): UNTILN(4)<>N(1)
      AND N(4)<>N(2) AND N(4)<>N(3)
260   REPEAT: N(5)=RND(5): UNTIL
      N(5)<>N(1) AND N(5)<>N(2) AND
      N(5)<>N(3) AND N(5)<>N(4)
270   ENDPROC
280   DEFPROCintro
290   PRINT' 'TAB(6)"Watch carefully."
300   PRINT'TAB(6)"Try to remember the
      order"
310   PRINTTAB(6)"in which the colours
      appear."
320   PRINT"TAB(6)"Press space bar"
330   A=GET:PRINTTAB(6,5)SPC(255)
340   ENDPROC
350   DEF PROCinput
360   FOR T=TO 5
370   INPUT A$(T)
380   PROCcheck
390   IF colour<>N(T) PROCwrong
400   NEXT T
410   PRINT' "You scored ";5-WRONG;" out
      of 5."
420   IF WRONG=0 PRINT' "Well done."
430   PRINT' "Press space bar."
440   ENDPROC
450   DEF PROCcheck
460   colour=0
470   IF A$(T)="R" THEN colour=1
480   IF A$(T)="G" THEN colour=2
490   IF A$(T)="Y" THEN colour=3
500   IF A$(T)="B" THEN colour=4
510   IF A$(T)="P" THEN colour=5
520   ENDPROC
530   DEF PROCwrong: WRONG=WRONG+1:
      PRINT"WRONG COLOUR": ENDPROC
```

Pronouns

Here are some words we use instead of writing naming words over and over again.

I	you	he	she	it	they	them	us
we	his	her	their	me	him		

Which of these words would you use if you were writing about these?

1 Your dad   he/his/him

2 Yourself _____

3 A dog _____

4 Your mum and dad's house _____

5 Our neighbours _____

6 Your friend Jane _____

7 Your friend Karl _____

8 You and a group of friends ___

9 Your teacher _____

10 A bike _____

Fill in the missing spaces in these sentences.

1 The telephone is ringing. Can _____ hear _____?

2 This is my pencil. Sarah gave it to _____.

3 The boy ran as fast as _____could.

4 I have no sandwiches left. John ate _____all.

5 There are two new children in our class. _____ are called Janet and Ian Jones.

6 _____ am sorry, but I can't play out.

7 Jason is the best footballer. _____always scores the goals.

8 Here is my new B.M.X. bike. _____ has got my name on _____.

Finish these sentences in an interesting way.

1 My name is Stacey Willis. I _____

2 Julie and I are good friends. We _____

3 The cat drank the milk, but it _____

4 The old lady was very pleased when she _____

5 The two burglars tried to escape. They _____

2.7a Skillmaster — pronouns
© Collins Educational 1990. ATs 1-4

Name_____

More Than One

When a word ends in **-y**, we make it more than one by leaving off the **-y** and adding **ies.**

daisy — daisies   fly — flies

Except when the letter before the **-y** is a vowel (a,e,i,o,u), then we just add an **s.**

turkey — turkeys   baby — babies

Make these words into more than one.

1 cry _____

2 story _____

3 toy _____

4 bay _____

5 way _____

6 key _____

7 stray _____

8 baby _____

9 sty _____

10 guy _____

11 Napoleon was the commander of huge _____ (army)

12 The _____ were very funny. (monkey)

13 _____ are churches. (abbey)

14 The _____ all wore diamonds and pearls. (lady)

15 The sun's _____ melted the snow and warmed the soil. (ray)

Make these words into more than one and write a sentence for each one.

1 (boy) _____

2 (dragonfly) _____

3 (country) _____

4 (tray) _____

5 (party) _____

2.7b Skillmaster — plurals
© Collins Educational 1990. AT4/3b

Name_____

Story Map

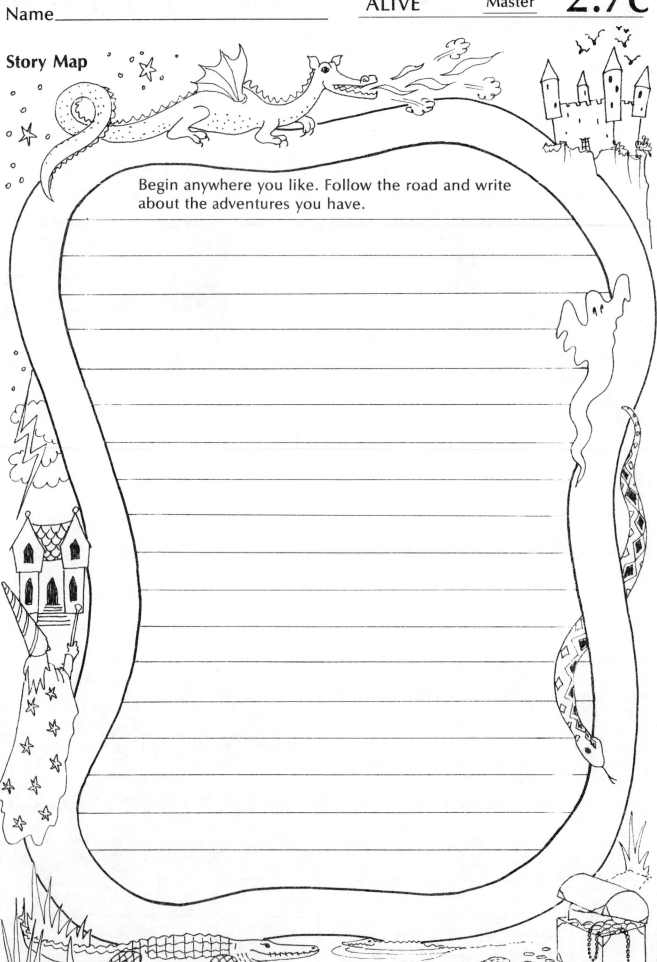

Begin anywhere you like. Follow the road and write about the adventures you have.

Name_____

ENGLISH
ALIVE

Level 2
Master

2.7d

Kim's Game

	A	B	C	D
1				
2				
3				
4				
5				

2.7d Kim's game
© Collins Educational 1990. ATs 1-4

Name_____

ENGLISH
ALIVE

Level 2
Master

2.7e

Listening

1 What did the speaker say?
   a) McKinley has scored a goal for City!'
   b) 'McKinley has scored a goal for United!'
   c) 'The goal has been disallowed!'
   d) 'What a goal — McKinley's done it again!'

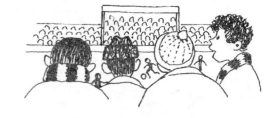

2 What did the announcer say?
   a) 'The train standing at platform 7 is running
       approximately ten minutes late.'
   b) 'The train standing at platform 8 is about to
       depart.'
   c) 'The train standing at platform 10 is running
       approximately 7 minutes late.'
   d) 'The train at platform 8 is going to King's Cross.'

3 What did the secretary say?
   a) 'There's a lady to see you, Miss Vines.'
   b) 'There's a gentleman to see you, Mr. Vines.'
   c) 'Here's your coffee, Mr. Vines.'
   d) 'There are two gentlemen to see you, Miss
       Vines.'

4 What did the man at the bus stop say?
   a) 'The number 56 bus is always late.'
   b) The number 96 bus is never late.'
   c) 'The number 96 bus is always late.'
   d) 'I do wish the 56 would hurry up!'

5 What did the girl at the disco say?
   a) 'I'm really thirsty. Are you?'
   b) 'Do you want a drink?'
   c) 'Shall we have a drink?'
   d) 'Let's go and get a drink.'

6 What did the man in the garage say?
   a) 'Get a move on, Joe, this tyre needs changing!'
   b) 'Hurry up, Bill, this exhaust needs changing!'
   c) 'Get a move on. This tyre needs changing!'
   d) 'Get a move on, Mike, this tyre needs
       changing!'

2.7e Figure/ground differentiation
© Collins Educational 1990. AT1/3b

Unit 8

Title — Pets
Theme — Animals
Stimuli — from *The Battle of Bubble and Squeak* by Philippa Pearce (Andre Deutsch);
from *Gone to the Dogs* by John Rowe Townsend (O.U.P.)

AT1 Speaking/listening
3a & c   developing an imaginary pet and its habits

ATs 1-4 Word skills
● receptacles
● adverbs of manner
● homonyms

AT2 Reading
"Battle of Bubble and Squeak":
3b-c & f   reading for the main idea:
3b-c & f   matching titles to paragraphs
3b-c & f   choosing the best title for passage
3b; d   cloze procedure
3f   reading for detail
3f   inference

"Gone to the Dogs":
3b-c   imaginative (pupil thinking herself into situation)
3b-c & f   reading for detail
3b-c & f   reading for the main idea
3d   inference

3f   bar chart — checking facts
3f   using a dictionary

AT3 Writing
3a   paragraph building — completing a second sentence and adding one or more sentences to make a paragraph
3a   writing sentences
3c & e   imaginative — child as a "pet" of some animals — making up an imaginary pet
3d   compiling a fact chart on pets (links with **2.8a**)
3d   bar chart of favourite wild animals

AT4 Maths
AT13   handling data
3a   construct and interpret bar charts

Science
AT1   Exploration of science
3f-g   bar charts — use and interpretation

Cloze passage:
The actual words used by the author are given here for reference only.
They should not be regarded as the correct answers — 1) caught   2) for   3) one
4) was   5) dropping   6) not   7) of
8) herself   9) with.

Activity sheets:
2.8a   receptacles **ATs 1-4**
2.8b   adverbs of manner (Skillmaster) **ATs 1-4; AT3/3a**
2.8c   pet chart for filling in **AT2/3f; AT3/3d**

Listening skills:
2.8d   Selection — using sound clues to trace routes on a plan (zoo) **AT1/3d; AT3/3b; AT3/3d**
Side 2, track 1.   Tape counter _____
This track gives an aural trip around a zoo using sound effects only. The pupil has to trace on a plan the route taken.

When the route has been marked the pupil is asked to write an account of his visit and the animals seen. This will require a separate sheet of paper.

Listening and speaking:
1   Pet Care. The children prepare a short speech on their own pet and how they look after it. If they do not have a pet of their own they may talk about one they would like to own.   **AT1/3a, b & d**

2   Talk about animals that work for us:
Dogs — police, mountain rescue, guard dogs, sheep dogs.
Horses — police, card horses, farm horses, racing horses.
Work animals in other countries — oxen, sled dogs, elephants etc.   **AT1/3b & d**

3   *Pretend Animals:* Arrange the children in groups of four or five. Each group should have a leader to start off the game. The leader describes the head of an imaginary animal. The description is

then passed round the group and other members add descriptions of the body, the front legs, hind legs and the tail. The description should be as hilarious as possible. When the description is complete the group should collectively think of a name for the animal. The activity may be completed by the children drawing a picture of the animal described, trying to recall and record all the detail included in the description. Display the pictures as a Zany Zoo. **AT1/3c-d**

4 *Animal Consequences:* Play this game as a development of Pretend Animals, or as a stimulus for it. The children should be seated in a circle and each one given a piece of paper and a pencil. On the left side of the paper the first child draws the head of an animal, and then folds the paper so that only the edges of the drawing can be seen. The papers are then passed on. The neck is then drawn to connect with the head. The paper is then folded as before and passed on. This is repeated adding the fore-legs, the body, the hind legs and tail. Then a name for the animal is added. The papers are then unfolded and the results enjoyed and discussed, before being added to the Zany Zoo. **AT1/3c & d**

5 Talk about the idea of animals ruling the world, as in 'Planet of the Apes' and 'Gone to the Dogs'. Discuss how different kinds of animals would behave if given this power e.g. mice, wasps, crocodiles, cats, kangaroos etc. **AT1/3c**

6 Read aloud the stories written by the children about being the pets of animals. **AT2/3a**

Follow-up activities:

1 Begin a project on Animals. Collect photographs, pictures, postcards and books and set up a resource corner. Where possible bring real animals into this corner. Visit a zoo, safari park, farm or circus.

2 Make a collection of receptacles and their contents. These can range from everyday things such as envelopes, boxes, packets, cartons etc. to pictures of more unusual receptacles: barrel, hamper, carafe, oil tanker etc.

3 *Pets Word Chain:* Hold a competition among the children to see who can make the longest pets chain. The chain is made up of pets' names. The second name should begin with the last letter of the first name. If the names of wild animals are included the game is made a little easier:

cat — toad — dog — guinea pig — goat — tortoise — emu etc. **ATs 1-4**

4 Create a learning mobile. This can be done in two ways:
   a) Collectively: Each child thinks of an animal/pet and on a large piece of card an outline of the animal's shape should be drawn. Each child then uses both sides of cards as a word bank. Words to describe the animal, its movements, its parents, young, home, food etc. may be included. These can then be suspended to form an attractive and educational display. **ATs 1-4**
   b) Individually: Again each child selects an animal, but this time small card outlines are cut out and one word is put on each card. Each mobile therefore is separate and can have as many extra pieces as the children can think of. These mobiles can then be suspended to form a display. **ATs 1-4**

5 *Adverb Mimes:* The group is divided into two teams. Each member of the team performs a mime after announcing what he is going to do e.g. 'Turning slowly'. Points are given for how well the mime is performed. After the first round the mime should be performed without introduction and the points given only if the action and adverbs can be correctly identified. **AT1/3c**

Where are they kept?

wild animals
criminals
pupils
books
young trees and plants
cars
orphans
drinking water
rubbish
frozen food

prison
library
garage
zoo
school
dustbin
deep freeze
school
nursery
orphanage

What might you find in these?

suitcase _____ *clothes* _____

basket _____

brief case _____

tin can _____

packet _____

wardrobe _____

safe _____

carton _____

bottle _____

tank _____

barrel _____

cellar _____

handbag _____

bucket _____

jar _____

purse _____

kettle _____

vase _____

flask _____

sack _____

wallet _____

notebook _____

plant pot _____

glass _____

saucepan _____

jug _____

bowl _____

carrier bag _____

magazine rack _____

mug _____

envelope _____

shopping trolley _____

2.8a Receptacles
© Collins Educational 1990. ATs 1-4

Name_____

Words which describe how something is done

The man walked.   This tells us what the man did.
The man walked *slowly*.   This tells us *how* the man did it.

Words which tell us how something is done usually end in **-ly**.
Add **-ly** to these words.

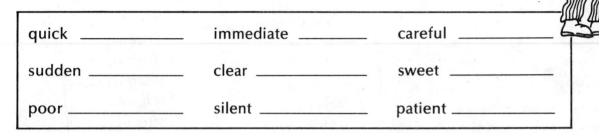

quick _____	immediate _____	careful _____
sudden _____	clear _____	sweet _____
poor _____	silent _____	patient _____

Choose one of these words for each of these sentences.

1   The thief ran _____ but he was still caught by the policeman.

2   The children waited _____ for the traffic to pass.

3   'Come here _____,' shouted the teacher.

4   The last horse fell _____ as it approached the last fence.

5   I can see _____ now that I have got my new glasses.

6   The waitress _____ carried the tray across to the table.

7   The birds were singing _____.

8   The boy was feeling _____. He had a bad cold.

Make up your own sentences using these words.

1   deeply _____

2   bravely _____

3   quietly _____

4   cruelly _____

5   smartly _____

6   lightly _____

7   bitterly _____

8   seriously _____

2.8b Skillmaster — adverbs of manner
© Collins Educational 1990. ATs 1-4; AT3/3a

Name_____

Pet Chart

Type of Pet/Name	Colour	Food	Where it sleeps	How it moves	Sounds

2.8c Pet chart
© Collins Educational 1990. AT2/3f; AT3/3d

Name_____

Using sound clues

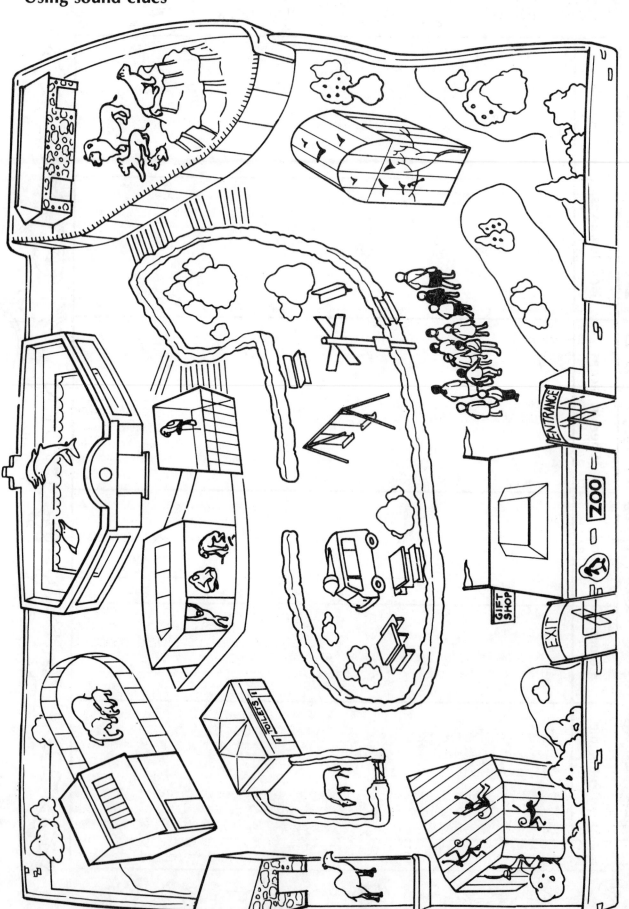

When you have listened to the tape, and drawn the route on the map, write an account of your visit, saying something about each animal.

2.8d Using sound clues
© Collins Educational 1990. AT1/3d; AT3/3d; AT3/3b

Unit 9

Title — Sky
Theme — The Sky
Stimuli — from *A Necklace of Raindrops* by Joan Aitken (Jonathan Cape); 'The Balloon' — Karla Kuskin from *In the Middle of the Trees*, (Harper and Row); also included in *Days Are Where We Live*, Jill Bennett (Bodley Head); from *The Giraffe and the Pelly and Me* by Roald Dahl (Jonathan Cape).

ATs 1-4 Word skills
- rhymes

AT2 Reading
3b-c & f   reading for the main idea
3b; d   context clues
3c   sequencing
3f   scanning for details
3f   following instructions: making a paper aeroplane

AT3 Writing
3c & e   imaginative, writer as spectator
3c & e   imaginative and descriptive, writer as participant
3d & e   detailed instructions for making something
3d & e   recording observations of paper plane experiments
3d & e   creating magic sweets and designing wrappers for them

Science
AT1   Exploration of Science
3a   formulate hypotheses
3h   interpret general observations

Activity sheets:
2.9a   listing ingredients in order used listing utensils **AT2/3f**
2.9b   recipe — flow diagram **AT3/3b**

Listening skills:
2.9c   selection — attention to detail — identifying places from spoken clues
Side 2, track 2. Tape counter _____

This sheet contains nine pictures of places. The voice on the tape describes four locations which should be numbered as they are identified by the child. The places are: 1) supermarket   2) park   3) airport 4) church. **AT1/3c-d, AT3/3d**

2.9d   aural memory — sequencing pictures from sound clues **AT1/3c-d; AT2/3d**
Side 2, track 3. Tape counter _____

This sheet should not be filled in until after the children have listened to the tape, which contains a story in sound of a boy's cycling trip to the beach. The children are then asked to sequence eight pictures to show the places in the order he visited them.

1   setting off from home
2   light traffic on road
3   pelican crossing
4   cycling through woods
5   cycling past farm
6   tractor
7   bridge over stream
8   lying on beach, looking at sky

Listening and speaking:
1   *Where Am I?*
Each child describes a place for other children to identify. **AT1/3c-d** (See **2.9c**)

2   *Rhyme Time*
The children sit in small groups of four or five. Each group is then given a word to start with e.g. *day, hit, high* etc. Each member of the group must in turn supply a rhyming word for the given word. Any child who fails to do so, or repeats a word already given, is out.
  More difficult words can be given as the children become more proficient. **AT1/3c-d**

3   *Tell Me How*
Each child has to describe how to do a simple everyday action e.g. brushing teeth, washing the dishes etc. He must do this without using his hands or making any gesture. **AT1/3c-d**

4   *The Balloon Game*
A balloon is slowly sinking towards a shark-infested sea. The four passengers are, for example, a pop singer, a doctor, a teacher and a policeman. One of them must jump in order to save the others. Each one has just a few minutes to show that he is too important to be sacrificed. The rest of the group should listen to each speech in turn and then vote on who should jump. Their discussion should be based purely on

the merits of the speeches heard.

The game may then be repeated with other occupations. **AT1/3b, c & d**

Follow-up activities:

1 *Rhyming Word Webs*

Provide large word webs in the classroom which children can add to as they discover new rhyming words. When the webs are full the centre word may be changed and the activity repeated. **ATs 1-4**

2 *Further Experiments with Paper Aeroplanes*

a) Bend the nose of the plane to one side. What happens? Try to explain why. (Science **AT1/3a, d, i**)

b) Make paper planes of different sizes. Which size flies best? (Science **AT1/3a, d, i**)

c) Make darts from different types of paper: newspaper, tissue paper, card, cartridge paper, etc. Test them to see how far they will fly. Record the results. (Science **AT1/3a, d & i**)

Design a fair test for deciding the best long-distance flyer e.g. The average distance travelled after three flights. This brings in Maths work. (Science **AT1/3c**) **AT1/3c**

d) Does the design of the plane affect its flight? (Science **AT1/3a & b**) Allow the children to design and construct their own paper planes after experimenting with all the variables mentioned above. Ask them to think of a name for their plane and then to produce detailed instructions for its construction and launching. **AT1/3c-d**

e) Stage a flying competition. Categories may be: longest flight, most spectacular aerobatics, most accurate landing in a set area etc. Allow the children to discuss and decide upon a fair test for each category, and how the results should be recorded. (Graph, table etc.) (Science **AT1/3f, g, h & i**) **AT1/3c**

f) Display the most successful planes alongside the instructions for making them. **AT3/3b**

3 *Skyscapes*

Use marbling techniques to produce interesting and original sky pictures:

Dark blues: night sky
Pale blue/white: cloud sky
Orange/red: sunrise/sunset
Silhouettes in black mounted on top of the marbling make the results even more effective and dramatic.

4 *Cloud Watching*

Take the children outside on a suitable day and let them watch for clouds. Can they 'see' anything in the clouds? Do the shapes remind them of anything. Follow this up by making cloud ink-blots on blue paper with white paint. A close examination of the results provides ideas for creative writing.

5 *Bird Watching*

Go outside and watch birds flying. Notice their movements and speed. Compare different birds and think of words to describe their ways of flying. **AT1/3c**

6 Follow up the work on paper aeroplanes by designing and building a kite.

7 *Poems:* **AT2/3b & c**

'Clouds' — Aileen Fisher, *In the Woods, In the Meadow, In the Sky*, World's Work Ltd.

'A Piece of Sky' — Julie Holder, included in *A Third Poetry Book*, Oxford.

'The Sun is Stuck' — Myra Cohn Livingston, *A Crazy Flight and Other Poems*, Harcourt Brace Jovanovich Inc.

'Sunset' — Mbuyiseni Oswalt Mtshali, *Sounds of a Cowhide Drum*, Oxford

'Summer Full Moon' — James Kirkup

'Starfish' — Judith Nichols

(Both included in *A Fifth Poetry Book*, Oxford)

'The Red Kite' — Lillian Moore, *I Thought I Heard the City*, Atheneum

'Jigsaw Puddle' — Emily Hearn, included in *Days Are Where We Live*, compiled by Jill Bennet, Bodley Head

'Flying' — J. M. Westrup

'The Moon That Broke' — Jeanette Ratcliffe

'Moon Magic' — Pamela Tennant

(All three are included in *Poetry Plus 4*, Schofield & Sims Ltd.)

'Boy Flying' — Leslie Norris

'I wonder how much air there is in this balloon?' — O. O'Neill

(Both are included in *The Kingfisher Book of Children's Verse*)

Name_____

Jam Tarts

Ingredients

Any flavour of jam
(or even lemon cheese)
100g flour
50g lard
50g butter or margarine
pinch of salt
cold water

Method

1 Sieve the flour in a bowl. Add the salt.
2 Add the lard and butter and rub into the flour using the fingertips.
3 Rub the mixture until it looks like fine breadcrumbs.
4 Add just enough water to hold the pastry together.
5 Make the dough into a ball and place on a lightly floured surface.
6 Lightly flour a rolling pin and roll the pastry smooth and flat. (½cm thick.)
7 Use a pastry cutter to cut out pastry circles.
8 Put pastry circles into a lightly greased tart tray.
9 Add 1 teaspoon of jam to each tart.
10 Bake in hot oven for 15-20 minutes, or until pastry is golden brown.

CAREFUL! Allow the pastry to cool completely before eating. The jam can get very hot.

1 Write down the ingredients in the order they are used.

_____

_____

_____

_____

_____

_____

2 Make a list of all the equipment used in making the tarts.

_____

_____

_____

_____

2.9a Recipe
© Collins Educational 1990. AT2/3f

Name_____

ENGLISH
ALIVE

Level 2
Master

2.9b

Making Jam Tarts — 2

Flow Chart
Read the recipe on sheet **2.9a** again. Complete this flow chart.

Sieve flour. Add salt.

Rub lard and butter into flour.

Rub until mixture is like

Add water to hold

Roll into a

Cut

Place

Add

2.9b Flow chart
© Collins Educational 1990 AT3/3b

Name_____

Where Am I?

On the other side of this sheet write a description of two places you know well. Do not name them. See if your friend can recognise them.

2.9c Attention to detail
© Collins Educational 1990. AT1/3c-d: AT3/3d

Name_____

ENGLISH
ALIVE

Level 2
Master

2.9d

Off to the Beach

What do you think Carl is dreaming of?
Do you ever have dreams when you look up at the sky?
Write your answers on the other side of this sheet.

2.9d Sequencing pictures
© Collins Educational 1990. AT1/3c-d; AT2/3d

Unit 10

Title — Fears
Theme — Fears
Stimuli — from *Danny the Champion of the World* by Roald Dahl (Jonathan Cape);
'The Silent Spinney' by Seamus Redmond, included in *A First Poetry Book*, (Oxford).

AT1 Speaking/Listening
3a & c	projecting into the experiences of others
3c	reactions to horror films
3c	reflecting on own feelings

ATs 1-4 Word study
● word building — full words

AT2 Reading
3b & d	cloze procedure
3b & d	finding facts
3b & d	context clues
3b-c & e	reading for the main idea
3b-d	reading reports and drawing bar charts
3c-d	imaginative response to passage
3d	inference
3f	using a dictionary

AT3 Writing
3a	writing two- or three-sentence paragraphs
3c & e	imaginative story based on the extract from "Danny the Champion of the World"
3c & e	writing and painting a picture about a nightmare
3d & e	letter of complaint to a newspaper
3d & e	making bar charts to show results of research into the greatest fears of the class

Maths
AT13
3a	bar charts

Science
AT1
3f & g	bar charts

Activity sheets:
2.10a revision of joining sentences (Skillmaster)
(using *and*, *but*, *who*, *which*, *because*) AT3/3a
2.10b group prediction *Spottimilitis* — 1 AT1/3c; AT2/3c-e
2.10c group prediction *Spottimilitis* — 2 AT1/3c; AT2/3c-e
2.10d group prediction *Spottimilitis* — 3 AT1/3c; AT2/3c-e
2.10e group prediction *Spottimilitis* — 4 AT1/3c; AT2/3c-e

Speaking and listening skills:
1 Talk about the different fears the children have and discuss the different levels of fear:— nervousness, excitement, guilt, conscience, phobias, nervous allergies, asthma, loneliness etc. Make the children aware that adults are frightened by similar things to those which frighten children. AT1/3c

2 Discuss the different phobias people may have and try to find their names e.g. *agoraphobia* — fear of open spaces
claustrophobia — fear of enclosed spaces
hydrophobia — fear of water
arachnaphobia — fear of spiders
AT1/3c

3 Talk about incidents which might have caused these fears e.g. a fear of water may be the result of being pushed into a river in early childhood. AT1/3b & c

4 Discuss possible actions that can be taken to overcome fears e.g. hypnotism, use of drugs etc. AT1/3c

5 What do the children do when scared?
e.g. hide head in a cushion
hide under bedclothes
hold mum/dad's hand
whistle etc. AT1/3d

6 Discuss the difference between things the children enjoy being frightened by and those that genuinely terrify. AT1/3c

7 Discuss the importance of fear: why it is necessary to run away from certain dangers? AT1/3c

Follow-up work:
1 Draw pictures of things the children enjoy being frightened by e.g. ghosts, witches etc.

2 Make lists of the things which frighten the class. Write a sentence for each one. **AT3/3d**

3 Combine the results of the class's reports on the things they are afraid of, and make a bar chart. (Science **AT1/3f, g & h**; Maths **AT13/3a) AT3/3d**

4 Collect pictures/posters of horror movies to make a montage of monsters or a Hall of Horrors.

5 Let the children make up a horror story and act it out, either as a serious story or as a spoof. **AT1/3c**

6 Make pictures of the haunted house scenes by using marbled backgrounds and black sugar paper for silhouettes.

7 Make a *Word Wall* display to show the different words used to express fear:

fright	scare	horror
tremble	quake	quiver
tense	jumpy	horrify
worry	anxious	phobia
fear	lonely	nervous
terror	terrify	etc.

ATs 1-4

8 Examine a vocabulary display of *-ful* words. Note the spelling rule change in beautiful and awful. **AT4/3c**

9 Many people are afraid of being alone. What makes people lonely? **AT1/3c** How does it feel to be lonely? Write poems about fear or loneliness. **AT3/3c** Here is a 'blueprint':

Fears
I feel scared when I ....
And when I ....
And if I'm ....
My biggest fear is ....
And ....
When I'm scared I ....
Or I .... or even ....
And that makes me feel ....

10 Read the *Who's Afraid?* series of books by Richard Carlisle (Orbis).
Who's Afraid of Monsters?
Who's Afraid of the Dark?
Who's Afraid of Spiders?
Who's Afraid of Ghosts? **AT2/3a & b**

11 Write letters of complaint about local and topical issues. **AT3/3d**

Name_____

Joining Sentences

Join these sentences using **and, but** or **because.**

1 The soldier took careful aim. He fired at the enemy.

_____

2 Mumtaz was not allowed near the water. She could not swim.

_____

3 John does not believe in ghosts. He does believe in witches.

_____

4 I'm going home. It's time for my tea.

_____

Join these sentences using **who** or **which.**

1 The vampire opened the coffin lid. It creaked noisily.

_____

2 The boys congratulated the footballer. He had scored all the goals.

_____

3 The skeleton frightened the girl. She ran away screaming.

_____

Join these sentences with **and, but, who, which** or **because.**

1 We found a group of people. They were lost.

_____

2 I looked out of my window. I could see a car.

_____

3 I was very tired. I could not get to sleep.

_____

4 Alison looked at the sky. It was very cloudy.

_____

5 The clock struck midnight. It was really only six o'clock.

_____

Spottimilitis: Part 1

On Monday morning Gareth woke up and decided he did not want to go to school.

'I'll only get into trouble as usual,' he thought to himself. 'If only I were sick or something!' But he wasn't and that was that. Or was it?

'Mum, I've got a headache,' he moaned when she came to get him out of bed.

'So have I, dear,' she replied, and that was all the sympathy he received from her.

Later that day as he was sitting in class colouring a picture with felt-tip pens and feeling sorry for himself, an idea came to him: an idea that would make his mum sit up and take notice. The next morning he woke up early and took out his pack of felt-tip pens. He disappeared into the bathroom, and after a few minutes went back to bed to await his mother.

'Mum, I feel most peculiar,' he moaned as she drew back the curtains.

'So do I, dear,' came her usual reply. Then she stopped and looked at him. A ray of sunlight shone on a crop of bright red spots all over his face. She came over and looked at him closely.

'How do you feel?' she asked, deeply concerned.

'Headache, and sore throat,' he said in a pathetic voice.

'I'm going to call the doctor,' she decided.

'Does that mean I'm going to miss school?

'I'm afraid so, dear,' she replied.

'Oh, bother!' sighed Gareth, falling back onto the pillow with a look of despair on his face. When his mother had gone to phone the doctor, Gareth began to laugh quietly. After a few minutes the smile began to disappear from his face. He was becoming worried about the spots. They had fooled his mother, but would they fool the doctor?

To think and talk about

Here are some suggestions which a group of children made about the story.

Sarah: I think the doctor will know immediately that the spots aren't real.

Liam: Don't forget that the story is called *Spottimilitis*. I think that Gareth really will become sick.

Nicola: Yes, and then nobody will believe him, because he's told lies before.

Paul: I think he's going to get away with it. Otherwise it wouldn't be much of a story.

Which of these ideas do you agree with? Which do you think is the most likely? Have you any other ideas about what might happen next?

2.10b   Group prediction — 1
© Collins Educational 1990. AT1/3c; AT2/3c-e

Name_____

Spottimilitis: Part 2

About eleven o'clock that morning the door bell rang. Gareth swept aside the toys he had been playing with on the bed. He lay back on the pillow and tried to look really ill.

'This is Doctor Jennings, Gareth,' his mother announced as the doctor stepped forward. 'Our usual doctor is on holiday.'

'Hello, Gareth,' smiled the doctor, and then set about examining him. He looked long and carefully at the spots and Gareth began to feel really uncomfortable. Then the doctor looked down his throat, and took his temperature.

'Well is he going to be all right?' asked Gareth's mother.

Doctor Jennings looked at Gareth with a serious look on his face and then turned to his mother.

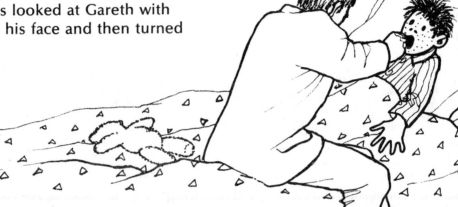

'I'm afraid what we've got here is a case of Spottimilitis.'

'Spottimilitis,' she echoed, 'what's that?'

'It's a very rare disease. In fact this is the first case I've come across.'

'But is it serious?'

'It can be,' replied the doctor, 'if left untreated. But don't worry. If you follow my treatment to the letter he should recover completely. I'll give you some medicine.' He took a bottle out of his bag. 'Horrible, nasty stuff I'm afraid, but it's the only cure. Two tablespoons every hour. And this room must be kept completely dark, and as quiet as possible, no music, no television, no excitement.' Gareth listened to all this in horror.

'I'll call back this evening and see how he is. Cheer up, Gareth,' he said. 'We'll have you up and about in ten days or so!'

The rest of the day was absolutely horrible. Gareth had never tasted such nasty medicine.

'I've got to do something about this,' he decided after the second dose. 'The spots must go.'

He began to wash them off a few at a time so his mother would not suspect anything.

To think and talk about:
1 Were you surprised at the doctor's diagnosis? Say why.
2 How would you feel if you were Gareth?
3 What do you think will happen when his mother sees the spots are disappearing?
4 What do you think the doctor will say?
5 Do you think Gareth will tell them the truth?

2.10c Group prediction — 2
© Collins Educational 1990. AT1/3c; AT2/3c-e

Spottimilitis: Part 3

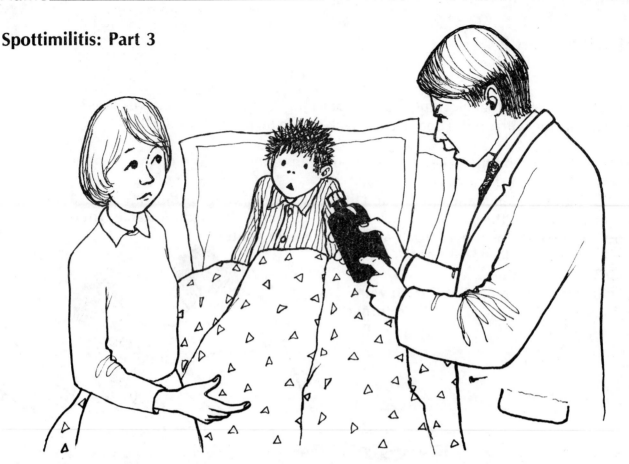

'You know, I do believe your spots are disappearing! she said as she gave Gareth his fifth dose of medicine. 'I wonder what Doctor Jennings will say about that?'

'So do I,' thought Gareth.

By the time the doctor arrived most of Gareth's spots had been carefully washed off.

'I'm feeling much better now,' Gareth told him.

Doctor Jennings looked puzzled and, to Gareth's surprise, rather worried.

'What is it, Doctor?' asked Gareth's mother anxiously.

'It's a lot more serious than I thought,' he said in a voice so soft that Gareth had to listen hard.

'But his spots are going, and he feels much better!' she protested.

'This morning he had all the symptoms of Spottimilitis,' explained the doctor, 'but the spots should have taken four or five days to clear. I'm afraid such rapid fading means only one thing: Gareth has not got ordinary Spottimilitis, but German Spottimilitis, an altogether rarer and more serious disease.'

Gareth's mother was most upset.

'Does that mean he will have to go into hospital?' Gareth listened in horror.

'Oh, no,' Doctor Jennings consoled her, 'not if you follow my instructions. He can continue taking the same medicine, but increase the dose to three tablespoons, every half hour. What a pity his spots had to disappear!'

Gareth now looked distinctly ill.

To think and talk about:
1   Did you find the doctor's reaction surprising? Why?
2   What do you think Gareth will do now?
3   How do you think the story will end?

2.10d   Group prediction — 3
© Collins Educational 1990. AT1/3c; AT2/3c-e

Spottimilitis: Part 4

'This can't go on any longer!' thought Gareth, but he could not face telling his mother and Doctor Jennings the truth. He took a desperate decision.

When his mother came to give him his next dose of medicine, Gareth seemed excited.

'It's not German Spottimilitis after all!' he said, 'Look my spots are coming back!' His mother looked at a new crop of red spots on his face and seemed puzzled.

'I'll ring Doctor Jennings,' she said. About an hour later the doctor arrived again.

'What's all this?' he asked.

'My spots are back,' smiled Gareth. 'It's ordinary Spottimilitis after all!' Doctor Jennings came over to his bed and looked at him.

'Gareth,' he began with a most serious expression on his face, 'I want you to be very brave. The return of your spots means you have Galloping German Spottimilitis. I'm afraid you'll have to go into hospital!'

Tears sprang to Gareth's eyes. He would have to tell them now. Then as his tears rolled down his face he saw his mother and the doctor were laughing.

'You know what you've really got?' laughed the doctor.

'Galloping German Spottimilitis?' said Gareth.

'No, felt-tip pen streaks all down your face!' His mother and the doctor fell about laughing.

'You knew all along, didn't you?' said Gareth.

'Yes, we knew, but we thought we'd teach you a lesson,' smiled his mother.

'But that horrible medicine!' protested Gareth.

'Nasty, but harmless,' explained the doctor, 'and by the way, I'm not really Doctor Jennings, just plain Mr. Jennings.'

'A friend of your father's,' said his mother.

'But that medicine really did work,' said Mr. Jennings, 'You'll never have Spottimilitis again.'

He was right. Gareth never did.

To think and talk about:
1 Were you surprised by the ending?
2 Look back over the story. Imagine you are Gareth's mother. What would make you suspicious about Gareth's illness?
3 Now imagine you are Gareth. What things might make you suspicious about the doctor?
4 Were you amused by the story? Say why you liked or didn't like it.
5 Would you have ended the story differently?

2.10e Group prediction — 4
© Collins Educational 1990. AT1/3c; AT2/3c-e

Unit 11

Title — Writing and Printing
Theme — Writing and Printing
Stimuli — Chinese pictographs and their origin.

AT1 Speaking/listening
3c   dealing with problems in the imagination and seeing possible solutions

ATs 1-4 Word study
- homophones
- word building: adding *un-*

AT2 Reading
3b   finding facts
3d   interpreting pictographs
3d & f   inference
3f   interpreting the Morse code
3f   fiction books: alphabetical order
3f   finding out how many languages are spoken by the children/ teachers in the school. Recording findings as a graph

AT3 Writing
3d-e   expanding telegram stories
3d-e   creating telegram messages
3d-e   writing a Morse code message
3f   creating pictographs

Activity sheets:
2.11a writing Chinese pictographs **AT2/3f**
2.11b a simple rebus story to interpret **AT2/3d**
2.11c a rebus story entirely in pictures, to interpret and express in writing **AT2/3d**

Follow-up activities:
1 Chinese writing is written in columns that go down the page. It is read from right to left. Find other languages that read differently from ours e.g. Arabic, Hebrew. **AT2/3c**

2 Try copying a story in columns from right to left, or practise simple mirror writing.

3 Let the children make and decorate small clay inkpots. Using a brush and ink the children may then try to form chinese characters. (Activity sheet **2.11a**).

4 Learn to write and count to ten in Cantonese.

5 The Chinese use ideographs as well as pictographs. Ideographs are signs for ideas e.g. good, think, bright etc. These were often made by combining two pictographs. **AT2/3f**

good/love 好	= woman 女	+ child 子
think 思	= brain 田	+ heart 心
bright 明	= sun 日	+ moon 月
sit 坐	= 2 men 从	ground 土
forest 林	= trees 木	
East 東	= sun 日	emerging behind a tree 木

Ask the children to invent their own pictographs for ideas such as good, bad, clever etc. **ATs 1-4**

6 Make more pictograph messages, trying to make them more complicated. Can the children invent a short story using pictographs instead of words? (Activity sheets **2.11b**, **2.11c**) **AT2/3d**

7 Make more pictograph book titles for display in the library/reading corner. **AT2/3d**

8 Examine other ways of writing such as cunieform. Follow the history and development of writing from cave paintings to modern times. **AT3/3d**

9 Have the class copy a particular passage and note the differences in handwriting? Are they all easy to read? Why is this? **AT5/3a**

10 Repeat the above using different writing implements: quill, brush, pencil, crayon, ball point pen, fountain pen, typewriter, word processor/ printer. Display the results and allow the children to comment on the differences. Which styles do they prefer *a)* to read? *b)* to write?

11 Allow the children to use a photocopier, spirit duplicator etc. to see how multiple copies can be produced.

12 Experiment with the selection of different type settings that are available in Letraset and on dot-matrix computer printers.

13 Try printing a message with a John Bull printing outfit. How easy is it to use?

14 Visit a local newspaper/printers to see modern printing technology in action.

15 Collect different typefaces and styles from newspapers and magazines. Make them into a montage.

16 Find examples of illuminated manuscripts. Let the children illuminate their own initials.

17 Find out about the history of books. For whom were they intended? What was written in early books? How did things change when the printing press was invented? **AT2/3e**

18 Look at book covers. They usually have illustrations which give a good idea of what the book is about. Let the children design a book cover for a story they have written or for their favourite story. Show the children how to find out who has illustrated their favourite books. **AT2/3e**

19 Do some practical printing for some attractive art displays:

   a) *Polystyrene Block Printing*
   Polystyrene is easily cut to the right shape and prints with an interesting texture.

   b) *Comb Printing*
   Spread thick paint on a sheet of paper, and then comb it with a cardboard comb. Lay a clean sheet of paper over it to print the pattern.

   c) *Bubble Printing*
   Add a small amount of washing-up liquid to a pot of paint. Use a straw to blow bubbles until they are level with the top of the container. Place a piece of cartridge paper over the container and allow time for the bubbles to settle before removing it.

   d) *Leaf Prints*
   Choose leaves with strong outline shapes, or clearly visible veins. Paint them and press the leaves carefully onto paper.

   e) *Screen Prints*
   For the more adventurous make screen prints using simple paper stencils.

   f) *Potato Prints*
   Let the children carve the letters A H I M O T V W X and Y. When they then attempt the remaining letters they will soon realise the need to reverse them before printing with them.

   g) *Lino Prints*
   Cut out the design using lino cutting tools. Ink the lino and print on paper to obtain a relief print.

20 Look at photographic prints and their negatives. Notice how the colours are reversed.

21 Send messages in Morse code using lights, or mirrors to reflect the sunlight. (Science **AT15/3a & b**)

22 Look at other sign languages: semaphore, or the deaf and dumb alphabet.

23 *Telegrams* **ATs 1-4**
Decide on a charge per word for a telegram message. Hold a class competition to see who can send the cheapest telegram version of a well-known story e.g. Cinderella. All the important details must be included.

24 *Something to think about!*
What does a Chinese typewriter or computer keyboard look like? How can it cope with all the different characters?

25 Follow up the work on homophones by using the computer program 'Some common Confusions'. This is available together with 'What is a Sentence?' on a single disc. Please see the appendices for more details of these and other programs in the Collins Educational series *Adventures in English*. **ATs 1-4**

Name_____

ENGLISH
ALIVE

Level 2
Master

2.11a

Chinese Pictographs

Use a fine paint brush to copy these pictographs for the numbers 1 to 10.
The arrows and numbers show the direction and order of each brush stroke.

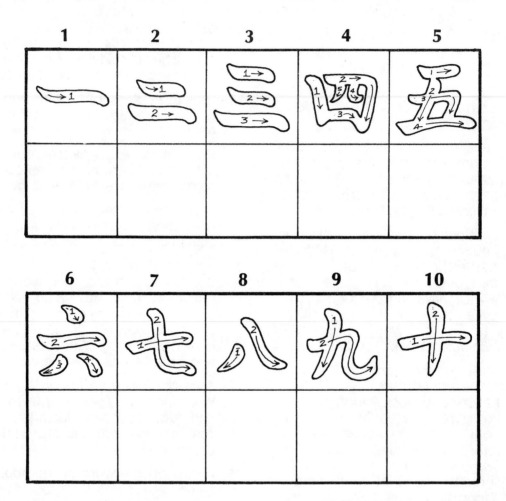

Look back at the Chinese pictographs in Unit 11. Draw the pictograph for each of these:

1 man	2 horse	3 woman
4 moon	5 tree	6 mountain

2.11a Chinese pictographs
© Collins Educational 1990. AT2/3f

Name_____

Rebus

Read this story carefully and then write it in your own words.

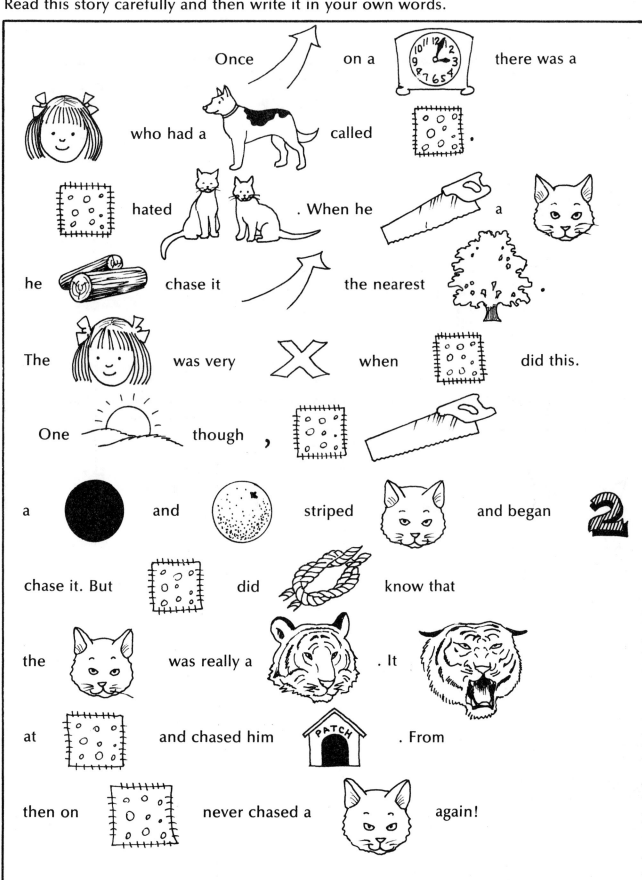

Name_____

The Clever Fox

Read this story carefully. Then write it in your own words on a separate sheet of paper.
Can you write a story like this, which only uses pictures?

2.11c   Rebus story
© Collins Educational 1990. AT2/3d

Unit 12

Title — Chit-Chat Magazine
Theme — A Magazine
Stimuli — Private? No! — Willard R. Espy, from *Another Almanac of Words at Play* (Andre Deutsch);
'Kidnapped!' — Shel Silverstein, from *A Light in the Attic* (Jonathan Cape);
The Ghost of Newby Church — originally entitled *A Ghost on Film* — Roderick Hunt, from *Ghosts, Witches and Things like that . . .* (Oxford).
The entire unit takes the form of a magazine.

AT1 Speaking/listening

Readers' Letters
3c   discussing controversial letters

ATs 1-4 Word study

Double Words:
- identifying double words e.g. book worm, watch-dog etc. from pictures
- illustrating similar words

AT2 Reading

Contents:
3f   re-organising parts of a contents list into alphabetical order and page number order
3f   skimming to spot errors in alphabetical order

The Smash Street Kids
3c-d   supplying suitable words for speech bubbles
3c-d   prediction

The Ghost of Newby Church:
3c-d   literal/inferential/imaginative

Look Into the Past — photograph of a class in 1913
3d   speculation
3f   making comparisons and contrasts with today

AT3 Writing

Contents
3c-e   choice of writing a story, a poem, an article or a review

Private? No!
3a   altering punctuation to change meaning

Readers' Letters
3d   writing replies to controversial letters
3d   writing a letter about any interesting topic

Kidnapped!
3c & e story or poem giving an amusing and completely unbelievable excuse for being late for school

Readers' Poll
3d   facts about self, favourite articles in "Chit-Chat" and ideas to make the magazine more interesting (Activity master 2.12a links with this.)

Activity sheets:

2.12a   questionnaire — Readers' Poll sheet for use with the Readers' Poll section in Unit 12 **AT3/3d**
2.12b   ideas sheet for a school or class magazine **AT3/3a-e**
2.12c   book report (fiction: Level 2) **AT2/3c-e**
2.12d   dictionary — guide words **AT2/3f**

Listening skills:

2.12e   aural memory — recall of detail
Side 2, track 4.   Tape counter _____

This track features an interview with a (fictitious) Olympic gold medallist. It is intended that the multi-choice question sheet should be given after listening to the interview, or turned face down during it.
The correct answers are: 1) a   2) c   3) a   4) b   5) c   6) a   7) a   8) b.

As follow-up work the children are asked to use the facts on the sheet to write an article for Chit-Chat magazine. **AT1/3c-d; AT3/3b**

Speaking and listening:

1   Discuss the magazines the children read.
Which is the most popular and why?
How many do they buy and how many do they borrow or exchange? **AT1/3c**
Which magazines/comics are more popular with boys than girls? Why?
What would be the ideal boys' magazine contain? Or the ideal girls' magazine?
AT1/3c

2   Use ideas sheet **2.12b** to discuss writing a class or school magazine. **AT1/3c;**

AT3/3d

3 Discuss famous people and the questions the children would like to ask them. Write these questions down and discuss what sort of answers the celebrities might give.

The children take it in turn to be a famous person. The rest of the group then ask them questions.

Record an interview with the most successful of these 'celebrities'. **AT1/3c-d**

Follow-up activities:

1 Make a graph of the magazines and comics read regularly by the children. **AT3/3d**

2 Make a graph of the money spent on them. **AT3/3d**

3 Set up a Swop Shop in the classroom for magazines.

4 Make a display of favourite articles and magazine items, together with a review for each one. **AT3/3d**

5 Ask the children to write a review of their own favourite magazine in order to tempt other children to read it. The new readers could then write their own views about it. **AT3/3d**

6 Write letters to real magazines. **AT3/3d**

7 Use the Level 2 fiction book review pro forma (**2.12c**). **AT3/3b & d**

8 Use the reference library to find material for a magazine article. **AT2/3f, AT3/3d**

Give each child a topic. He then has to find a picture about it to copy and colour. He must also write a few interesting sentences about his topic.

Ask him to write down the title and author of the books he found useful and to give page references.

The finished articles can be pasted into a magazine booklet.

Name_____

Chit-Chat Readers' Poll

The editor of *Chit-Chat* would like to hear your ideas on the magazine.
Please fill in the poll form and hand it to your teacher.

ABOUT YOU

Name _____

Address _____
_____

Age _____

School _____

Hobbies _____

Other interests _____
_____

ABOUT CHIT-CHAT

Do you like *Chit-chat*? _____

_____ Why/why not? _____

Which is your favourite *Chit-Chat* feature? _____

Why do you like it?_____
_____
_____

YOUR IDEAS TO MAKE CHIT-CHAT EVEN BETTER

What would you like to read about in *Chit-Chat*?
_____

How would you make *Chat-Chat* better? _____
_____
_____

2.12a Questionnaire
© Collins Educational 1990. AT2/3f

Your own magazine

Writing your own magazine is not hard if everybody helps.

1 Here are some of the things found in most magazines.
   Add any ideas of your own.
2 Discuss with the class the items you would like in your magazine.
3 Decide who is to write, draw, or paint each of these items.
4 When the items are ready decide which pages to put them on.
5 Paste them into a book, or mount them as a wall display.

▶▶ NEWS ◀◀

School events _____
Trips and holidays _____
Open days _____
Sports _____
_____
_____

▶▶ PICTURES and PHOTOGRAPHS ◀◀

The front cover _____
Paintings _____
Drawings _____
Photographs of _____
school events _____
Puzzle pictures _____
Cartoons _____

▶▶ REVIEWS ◀◀

Books _____
Plays and concerts _____
School meals _____
_____
_____
_____

▶▶ SPECIAL FEATURES ◀◀

Hobbies _____
Your school _____
Your neighbourhood _____
People _____
Places _____

▶▶ FUN ITEMS ◀◀

Jokes _____
Riddles _____
Limericks _____
Crosswords _____
Word Search _____
_____

▶▶ READERS' VIEWS ◀◀

Letters _____
Longer articles _____
What readers think _____
about your magazine _____

▶▶ STORIES and POEMS ◀◀

Adventure _____
Mystery _____
Comedy _____
Animals _____
Magic _____
_____

▶▶ COMPETITIONS ◀◀

Stories _____
Poems _____
Letters _____
Pictures _____
Photographs _____

2.12b Ideas for writing a class/school magazine
© Collins Educational 1990. AT3/3a-e

Name _____

Book Report

Title _____

Author _____

Publisher _____

The story is about _____

_____

_____

My favourite character is

because _____

_____

My favourite character	The most exciting part of the book.

Using the Dictionary — Guide Words

Open your dictionary somewhere in the middle. At the top of the page you will see two words.

The first word is the *first* word on that page for which a meaning is given.
The second word is the *last* word on that page for which a meaning is given.

Look at this example.

| try   twin |

The words which come between **try** and **twin** will be on this page.
tug, tulip, twenty and **twig** will all be on this page because the words in a dictionary are in alphabetical order.

1   Draw a ring round the words which would be found on this page.

tunnel	tank	train	treasure	turn	tune
Tuesday	type	twine	tree	tumble	tub

2   Draw a ring around the words which would be found between these guide words.

a) | lady   lastly |

laser	leaf	lead	lid	lamp	lane	landslide
lazy	label	lark	lack	law	land	lap

b) | skilful   sleeve |

spray	skulk	sleet	stop	slim	soft	sky
slam	same	seat	seaweed	slate	spot	stock

c) | vent   vet |

veteran	viola	value	very	vestry	vault	van
vessel	volcano	vulture	verb	verse	Venus	vest

d) | butter   camel |

cap	buy	brother	cold	call	buzz	canoe
calm	cape	button	butler	castle	card	cave

2.12d Dictionary — guide words
© Collins Educational 1990. **AT2/3f**

Name_____

Chit-Chat interviews Jason Lee

First listen to the interview on track 4, side 2
of the Level Two listening skills cassette.
Then answer the questions below.
Each question has three answers, but only
one of them tells what Jason Lee really said.
Underline each correct answer.

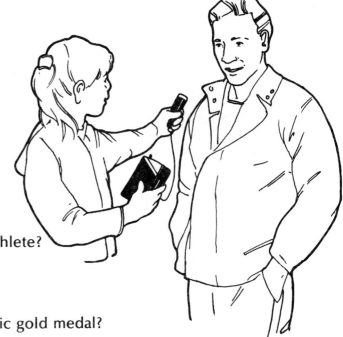

1 When did Jason Lee first decide to be an athlete?
   a) at primary school
   b) at secondary school
   c) at university

2 Over which distance did he win the Olympic gold medal?
   a) 1 500 metres
   b) 800 metres
   c) 3 000 metres

3 Who at primary school sometimes beat him?
   a) Christopher Mills
   b) John Appleton
   c) Lee Mills

4 Over which distance could the Olympic champion always win at primary school?
   a) 100 metres
   b) 800 metres
   c) 200 metres

5 Who organised his training?
   a) himself
   b) his teacher
   c) his father

6 Where did his training take place?
   a) in the country
   b) in the park
   c) at school

7 Was his school work affected?
   a) he didn't think so
   b) it was
   c) definitely not

8 What did Jason Lee say a runner needed, besides strong legs?
   a) powerful arms
   b) an active brain
   c) expensive running shoes

Use the information on this sheet to write an article about Jason Lee for *Chit-Chat* magazine.

2.12e Aural memory — recall of detail
© Collins Educational 1990. AT1/3c-d; AT3/3b

Unit 13

Title   — Talking and Listening
Theme — Talking and Listening
Stimuli — from *The Shrinking of Treehorn*
            by Florence Parry
            Heide (Puffin);
            from *The Sheep-Pig* by Dick King
            Smith (Puffin).

AT1 Speaking/listening
3a   role play
3a   reporting on past experiences
3c   reasoning

ATs 1-4 Word study
● collective nouns

AT2 Reading
3b-d   literal/inferential/imaginative
3c   sequencing
3d   reading for detail/supplying
        words for speach bubbles

AT3 Writing
3a   supplying words for speech
        bubbles
3a   inventing boasts (hyperbole)

3c   writing dialogue in dramatic form
        a class book of "Boasts"
3d   explanatory note
3d   making a list of things adults say

Activity sheets:
2.13a reading for detail/supplying words
        for speech bubbles **AT2/3d**;
        AT3/3a
2.13b writing dialogue in dramatic form
        AT1/3a; AT3/3a; AT2/3a
2.13c words of the same kind **ATs 1-4**

Listening skills:
2.13d following and re-telling the words
of a speaker **AT1/3d; AT2/3c; AT3/3b**
Side 2, track 5. Tape counter _____

A tray of rings has been stolen from a jeweller's shop. A policewoman arrives to question the jeweller.

The children are asked to supply from memory the information given by the jeweller. They should have the main points of the jeweller's account, but not necessarily the exact wording. However, the dialogue to be heard on the tape is given for reference.

WPC Atherton: Tell me what you can remember about the robbery.
Stevens: I was showing a young lady and gentleman a tray of diamond rings when a man suddenly pushed between them and grabbed the tray off the counter.
WPC Atherton: What did the man look like?
Stevens: He was wearing blue jeans and a red sweater.
WPC Atherton: Did he say anything?
Stevens: No, he just grabbed the tray and ran out of the shop. He bumped into a lady at the door and knocked her to the floor.
WPC Atherton: What happened then?
Stevens: Oh, yes. He was running hell for leather up the street and I set off after him, shouting 'Stop, thief!' He turned up an alley, but when I got there he was gone.
WPC Atherton: What did you do then?
Stevens: I came back to the shop and phoned you.
WPC Atherton: What was the value of the rings?
Stevens: About £7,000.

Speaking and listening activities:
1 Act conversations where an adult is not really listening to, or irritated by, a child. **AT1/3b & c**

2 *Telephone Conversations.* Discuss using a public phone box. Then act out different situations which require the making of emergency phone calls. **AT1/3c**
    Phone a friend to make arrangements for an activity at the weekend. One person answers the phone and pretends to be talking to a famous person. He must give out sufficient information for the rest of the group to identify that person.

3 *Hold a Boasting Competition.* The winner is the one who consistently makes the wildest and most amusing claims. **AT1/3c**

4 *Hold a Tongue Twisting Competition.* The group has to make up and read out tongue twisters. **AT1/3c**

5 *Hold a Tall Stories Competition.* The group have to make up and tell a tall story. The tallest story wins. **AT1/3c**

6 Read aloud conversation peoms such as Kit Wright's 'My Dad, Your Dad'

(Fontana). See also 'Further Reading'.
AT2/3a

7 *How Do You Say It?* Play this game as a stimulus or follow-up to the activity sheet **2.13c**. One member of the group thinks of a way of speaking e.g. mumbling, whispering, shouting etc. The rest of the group then gives him a sentence to say and from this to identify the word.

 A variation is for the speaker to think of an adverb and then speak the sentence in that manner e.g. quietly, angrily, jokingly etc. **ATs 1-4**

8 *How Do You Do It?* Here one member of the group thinks of an adverb and the rest of the group asks him to perform a series of actions in that manner until the adverb is identified. **ATs 1-4**

9 Collect and discuss everyday expressions about speaking. Here are some examples:
 None so deaf as those who will not hear.
 To send to Coventry.
 To blow one's trumpet.
 Tell it to the Marines.
 A cock and bull story.
 To blow one's top.
 To make a clean breast of it.
 The gift of the gab.
 To talk gibberish.
 to hold one's tongue.
 To bandy words.
 To chew the fat.
 ATs 1-4

Further Reading:
Not Now, Bernard — David McKee (Puffin)
Time to Get Out of the Bath, Shirley
Don't Go Near the Water, Shirley, both by John Burningham (Cape)
On the Way Home — Jill Murphy (Picturemacs/Macmillan) (tall stories)
The Kingfisher Book of Children's Poetry — selected by Michael Rosen
This book contains tongue twisters, and collected boasts as well as poems ideal for reading aloud and choral speech. Among those connected with this theme are:
 Irritating Sayings, collated by David Jackson
 All for an ice-cream, Karen Jackson
 Overheard on a Saltmarsh, Harold Monro
 What Some People Do
 AT2/3a

What are they saying?

Fill in each speech bubble.

You're not going to believe this!

Complete the following conversation.

Tony: You're not going to believe this!

Carl: Go on, try me.

Tony: Guess what happened in the park this morning!

Carl: You fell into the boating lake?

Tony: No. I saw _____

_____

_____

_____

Carl: What did you do then?

Tony: _____

_____

_____

_____

_____

Carl: That's nothing! Do you know what happened to me at the beach this morning?

Tony: You got chased by a shark?

Carl: Worse! _____

_____

_____

_____

_____

Tony: That's nothing! Did I ever tell you about my Uncle Harry in the jungle?

Complete this conversation on a separate sheet of paper. Then read it out loud with a friend.

2.13b Writing dialogue in dramatic form
© Collins Educational 1990. AT3/3a; AT2/3a; AT1/3a

Talk, Talk, Talk

Choose the word.

| whispered shouted asked mumbled exclaimed grumbled |

1 'Hello there,' he _____, 'can you hear me?'

2 'This just isn't fair,' she _____.

3 'Keep your voice down,' she _____, 'they might hear you.'

4 'That's really superb!' he _____.

5 We could not tell what he said because he _____.

6 'Is this the way to Manchester?' he _____.

Choose the word.

| word gossip speech interview conversation conference |

1 'I want a _____ with you, Treehorn,' said the Principal.

2 Gill made a _____ about the importance of telling the truth.

3 He had an _____ for a job as chief accountant.

4 There was a lot of _____ about our new neighbours, but none of it was true.

5 She had a long telephone _____ with her sister.

6 The leaders met for a _____ on pollution.

Name_____

The Snatch

Fill in the spaces with the words spoken by Mr. Stevens.

WPC Atherton: Tell me what you can remember about the robbery.

Stevens: _____

_____

_____

_____

WPC Atherton: What did the man look like?

Stevens: _____

_____

WPC Atherton: Did he say anything?

Stevens: _____

WPC Atherton: What happened then?

Stevens: _____

_____

WPC Atherton: Did you see which way he went?

Stevens: _____

_____

_____

_____

WPC Atherton: What did you do then?

Stevens: _____

WPC Atherton: What was the value of the rings?

Stevens: _____

On a separate sheet of paper write a similar interview with a woman who witnessed a road accident.

2.13d Following and retelling words of speaker
© Collins Educational 1990. AT1/3d; AT2/3c; AT3/3b

Unit 14

Title — Cops and Robbers
Theme — Cops and Robbers
Stimuli — from *The Willerbys and the Bank Robbers* by Pamela Oldfield (Blackie).

AT1 Speaking/listening
3a   projecting
3a   reasoning
3a   reporting on past experiences

AT2 Reading
Prose passage:

3b-c
 &f   reading for the main idea
3b & d context clues
3b & d cloze procedure
3c   retelling events from the points of view of different characters
3d   evaluation

Picture of bank robbery:
3f   studying picture details and answering questions from memory

Town Plan:
3f   using grid squares

Pictures of robbery and suspects:
3b-d   comparison of detail
3d   inference — looking for clues and reasoning from them
3d   speculation

AT3 Writing
3a   answering questions from memory
3b   recording contents of a passage from the points of view of two different characters
3b   recording an observed activity
3b-c   descriptive writing of events from picture clues; writer as participant
3d   recording observations and deductions

Cloze passage:
The actual words used by the author are given here for reference only. They should not be regarded as the correct answers —
1) nodded 2) People 3) staff 4) the
5) just 6) man 7) muttered 8) wonder
9) do 10) jeans 11) beginning.

Activity sheets:
2.14a reading for detail/logic **AT2/3c-d**
2.14b grid squares **AT3/3d**
2.14c group prediction *Strangers at the Grange* — 1 **AT3/3c; AT2/3c-e**
2.14d group prediction *Strangers at the Grange* — 2 **AT1/3c; AT2/3c-e**
2.14e group prediction — *Strangers at the Grange* — 3 **AT1/3c; AT2/3c-e**
2.14f group prediction *Strangers at the Grange* — 4 **AT1/3c; AT2/3c-e**

Speaking and listening:
1 *What Would You Do?* Discuss what the children would do if they saw an accident, a theft or any similar incident. Explore these situations in drama. **AT1/3b-d**

2 When might you need the help of a policeman. Make a list and use it to develop more situations for drama. **AT3/3d**

3 Discuss the difference between a policeman and a detective. **AT1/3c**

4 Discuss the qualities and skills needed by a good detective: observation, memory, patience, perseverence, clear thinking, accurate reporting, asking the right questions etc. **AT1/3c**

5 Discuss what is meant by a clue, evidence, a witness, an alibi, deduction and proof. **AT1/3c**

6 Ask a policeman to talk to the class about his work and the importance of detailed observation. Discuss in advance the aspects of his work the class would most like to learn about. **AT1/3c & d**

7 *Eye Witness:* An ideal follow up to the description of the theft in the Activities section of Unit 14. One group of children acts out a dramatic incident such as an accident. The other children have to watch carefully and describe what happened as accurately as they can. A video recording of the incident would help in checking the accuracy of the description. **AT1/3a-c**

8 Test the memory and powers of observation of the children by asking them to describe details of their everyday life:
e.g. what the head teacher is wearing today
descriptions of the teacher's cars
yesterday's weather

a recent class trip

what the children did last Saturday

AT1/3a & c

9 *Mystery Object:* The children take it in turn to describe an object which can be seen in the room. A list of attributes on the board will help: colour, size, shape, what it is made from, etc. The group should listen carefully to the complete description, and be discouraged from hasty guesses. If the object is not immediately identified from its description then the rest of the group may ask questions. **AT1/3c**

Follow-up activities:

1 *Observation and Memory*

Collect pictures from magazines of people and incidents and paste them on card. Give one to each child and ask them to write questions about the picture. Number the pictures and questions and issue them as required. The pictures may then be studied for a set time and then exchanged for the questions. **AT3/3d**

2 *Identikit Pictures*

These can be made quite simply by using a standard oval template for each child to draw round. The oval is then roughly divided into three equal parts: the top of the head, the eyes and nose, and the mouth. Each child then draws a face. The three parts may be identified by the child writing his name on the back of each part.

When all the faces are complete they can be mixed up and stored in three piles. The children will then enjoy sorting and matching features. Can they match up the original faces again?

The theme 'Detectives' will be explored further in Level 3.

Name_____

Whodunnit?

There has been a murder at Doomsbury Hall. The body of Daphne De Main has been found in the billiard room. She has been strangled and her diamond necklace stolen. *You* are the Detective Inspector sent to interview the suspects.

   Read what each suspect says about where he was and who he was with at the time of the murder. Then write the details on a separate sheet. The first one has been done for you.

Fiona Fortune: I was in the Hall with Angela Kane. We were just wondering where Lady Daphne was when we heard her scream.

Lady Kathryn: I was in the ballroom with Simon Simple.

Simon Simple: I was in the ballroom dancing with Lady Kathryn.

Colonel Crowther: I was in the Ballroom with Lady Kathryn when I heard the scream.

Angela Kane: I was with Fiona in the Hall. I'll have nightmares about it, I just know I will!

Lord Rutland: I was in the drawing room with Sir Peter Salt when I heard the scream.

Sir Peter Salt: I was in the drawing room with Lord Rutland when it happened.

Lady Rutland: I was alone in the library.

Name	Lord Rutland
Where?	Drawing Room
With?	Sir Peter Salt
Alibi checked with	Sir Peter Salt

I think the murderer is _____

because _____

_____

_____

On a separate sheet of paper
write an account of the murder.

2.14a Reading for detail/logic
© Collins Educational 1990: AT2/3c-d

Name_____

Map Squares

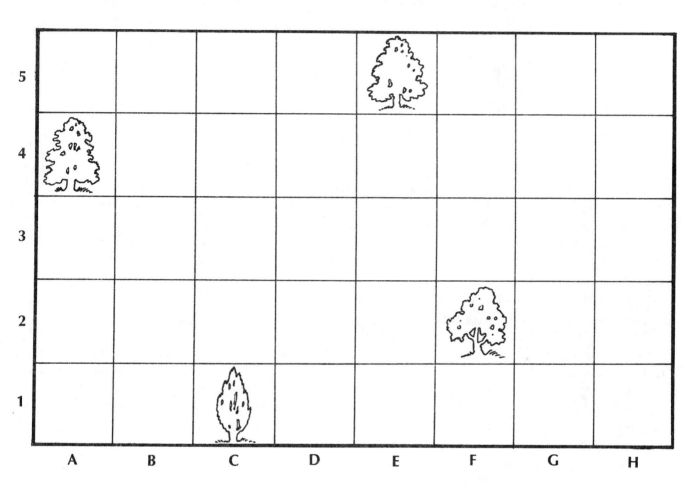

Look at the key. Put these items on the map:

1 A picnic area in square G5.
2 A pond in square B2.
3 A putting green in square B5.
4 A bridge in square D1.
5 A cafe in square D4.
6 A hill in square H5.
7 A tennis court in square G2.
8 Swings in square C3.

Key	
/∭\	swings
☕	cafe
⊓⊓	picnic area
🎾	tennis court
🏌	putting green
⌒	bridge
⬭	pond
⌒	hill

Thieves have buried their loot in this park,
but no one knows where. Where would you bury it?
Put a large 'X' in the square of your choice.

The treasure is now in square _____.

2.14b Grid squares
© Collins Educational 1990. AT3/3d

Strangers at the Grange: Part 1

Sue and Patrick walked past the Grange every day on their way to school. Sometimes they saw old Mrs. Cavendish at a window, or, more rarely, in the garden. On that particular day, however, she was not to be seen. They had already passed the house when their attention was attracted by raised voices. They turned back and looked through a gap in the fence. A young woman was arguing with a man on the lawn. He was holding a piece of paper in his hand.

'Just what were you thinking of?' she shouted angrily.

'Keep your voice down!' warned the man.

'You hit her too hard! Suppose she dies?'

'She's a tough old bird. She'll be all right,' said the man. He folded the paper and put it in his pocket.

'I'm going to call a doctor,' decided the young woman, turning towards the house.

'You'll do no such thing!' shouted the man. He grabbed the woman and twisted her arm. She hit him across the face and pulling away from him, ran into the house. The man followed her and the door slammed.

'What's going on?' Sue asked her brother.

'I don't know,' replied Patrick, 'but if we don't hurry up we'll be late for school.'

As they hurried along the path through the wood they discussed what they had seen.

'Who do you think they were?' asked Patrick.

'I've never seen them before,' replied Sue. 'I know that old Mrs. Cavendish has a daughter, but she lives in Australia.'

'Who do you think they are talking about?' asked Patrick, 'old Mrs. Cavendish?'

'I hope not! Do you think we should tell the police?'

'We'd feel silly if we were wrong,' said her brother.

To think and talk about:
1　What do you think is going on?
　　Who might the man and woman be?
　　Do you think anything has happened to Mrs. Cavendish?
　　Give reasons for all your answers.
2　What do you think Sue and Patrick should do next?
3　What do you think will happen next at the Grange?

2.14c Group prediction — 1
© Collins Educational 1990. AT1/3c; AT2/3c-e

Name_____

Strangers at the Grange: Part 2

The nearer Sue and Patrick got to school the less serious it all seemed. Yet at the end of afternoon school they hurried back through the woods to the Grange and looked through the hole in the fence.

A blue van was parked on the drive, but all was quiet. They waited for a few minutes, and were just beginning to lose interest when the door opened and the young woman stepped out. She looked all around and then said, 'All clear.'

Two men came out of the house carrying a stretcher. One of them was the man who had argued with her. Whoever was on the stretcher was completely covered with a blanket.

The woman went over to the van and opened the door. The men moved to slide the stretcher into the van. As they did so an arm dropped below the level of the blanket, and the woman quickly pushed it out of sight. The stretcher disappeared into the van and the door was locked.

'Stay here with the van,' said the first man. 'We'll give the house a final check.' He hesitated for a moment.

'The gun,' said the woman.

'The gun,' repeated the man, 'I think you'd better give it to me.'

The woman opened her shoulder bag and handed him a revolver. Patrick turned to his sister.

'Get the police!' he whispered urgently, 'I'll stay here and keep watch.' Sue nodded and hurried away in the direction of the village.

As soon as she had gone, Patrick moved softly along the fence to another hole which was just large enough for a boy to wriggle through. He crept forward towards the van. At that moment a dry twig snapped under his foot.

To think and talk about:
1 Have you changed your ideas about the story?
   What would you say is going on at the Grange?
   Give your reasons for thinking so.
2 What facts can Sue give to the police?
   Is it likely they will believe her?
3 What do you think will happen to Patrick?

2.14d Group prediction — 2
© Collins Educational 1990. AT1/3c; AT2/3c-e

Strangers at the Grange: Part 3

Ten minutes later a police car stopped outside the Grange. A policeman and policewoman got out and went up the drive with Sue.

'It's gone,' she said, 'the blue van has gone! And where's Patrick?'

The police looked all around, but there was no sign of either Patrick or the van. The policeman rang the door bell. When there was no answer he checked the doors and windows of the Grange. He could find nothing suspicious.

'I expect your brother has gone home for his tea,' said the policewoman.

'Come on we'll drop you off there.' Sue hesitated.

'No, it's all right I've got to call at the paper shop,' she said. She was bitterly disappointed. She set off slowly towards the village. When the police car had driven off, she turned back and began her own investigation. She walked all round the house, peering in through the windows.

After ten minutes she decided the police were right: Patrick had gone home to tea. She was moving round towards the front of the house, when there was the sound of a vehicle on the gravel drive. She flattened herself against the wall, and peeped round the corner. The blue van was back.

The man and woman who had argued that morning got out with a woman she had never seen before. All three went into the Grange. Sue crept along the wall, ducking under the windows as she went. She made only a little noise as she crossed the gravel towards the van. She looked in, but the van was empty.

The sound of angry voices came from the house. Then the door opened and the first woman came out of the house followed by the man.

'You hit her too hard! Suppose she dies?' screamed the woman. Sue crouched down behind the van.

'Not again,' she thought, 'please not again!'

To think and talk about:

1 How many different explanations can your group think of to explain what is happening?
   Which of these do you think is the most likely?
2 Was Sue wise to stay behind at the Grange?
3 What do you think has happened to Patrick?
4 How do you think the story will end?

2.14e Group prediction — 3
© Collins Educational 1990. AT1/3c; AT2/3c-e

Strangers at the Grange: Part 4

A large van turned into the drive. Sue saw the words *BBC TV* on the side. The man and woman stopped arguing and came over to the van. At the bottom of the drive a coach stopped. Someone was waving from it. Sue stood up and set off towards it at a run.

'Patrick!' she called, 'Where have you been. What is going on!' Patrick was grinning all over his face as he stepped from the coach.

'Look,' he said as he turned to help an old lady, 'it's Mrs. Cavendish!'

'But I don't understand,' protested Sue.

'It's all a play,' explained Patrick. 'Mrs. Cavendish has given permission to the BBC to film here at the Grange. The argument we saw was just a rehearsal, and the body on the stretcher was a dummy!'

The man and the young woman came over to join them.

'I hear we gave you a bit of a fright,' smiled the man. 'Sorry about that.'

'Why don't you run home and tell your mum where you are, and then come and have tea with us at the canteen van?' invited the young actress. 'Then we'll tell you all about it.'

Sue and Patrick needed no further invitation.

To think and talk about:

1 Were you surprised at the ending?
  Were you disappointed that no one was murdered?
  How would you have ended the story?

2 Look back over the earlier parts. How many clues can you find which show that the strange happenings at the Grange were really rehearsals for a film?

2.14f Group prediction — 4
© Collins Educational 1990. AT1/3c; AT2/3c-e

Unit 15

Title — Storm
Theme — Weather
Stimuli — from *Storm* by Kevin Crossley-Holland (Heinemann)
and from *A Song of Wind* by Will Lawson.

AT1 Speaking/listening
3a   reporting on past experience
3a & c   projecting — reflecting on feelings
3b   conveying a warning
3c   reasoning

ATs 1-4 Word skills
●   action words from poem "A Song of Wind"

AT2 Reading
"Storm" extract:
3b-c   appreciation
3b-c   finding facts
3b & d   cloze procedure
3d   inference

Weather symbols:
3b; d;   inference — matching symbols
f   to meaning

Beaufort Scale:
3b-c   finding facts
3b & f   main idea — matching pictures to wind force description

AT3 Writing
3c & e   description of a storm in prose or verse
3d & e   writing a poem, "A Song of Rain", using "A Song of Wind" as a model
3c & e   description of a gathering storm using information in the Beaufort Scale chart as a guide
3c & e   story writing on the subject "Storm", using a Make-a-Story chart

Science
AT9   Earth and Atmosphere
3e   understand media weather symbols

Cloze passage:
The actual words used by the author are given here for reference only. They should not be regarded as the correct answers —
1) never   2) great   3) looked   4) of
5) There   6) that   7) and   8) was   9) no.

Activity sheets:
2.15a   Assessment Master — cloze/adjectives/calendar **AT2/3d/f; ATs 1-4**
2.15b   Assessment Master — comprehension/past tense/joining sentences **AT2/3d; AT3/3a; ATs 1-4**
2.15c   Assessment Master — letter/description/narrative **AT3/3b-d**

Speaking and listening:
1   Are weather forecasts accurate? Note the local forecasts everyday for a week or more, and check them against the weather. What conclusions do you reach? **AT1/3c**

2   Discuss the truth of weather lore:
Red sky at night,
Shepherd's delight;
Red sky in the morning,
Shepherd's warning.
When the dew is on the grass,
Rain will never come to pass.
Rain before seven,
Fine after eleven.
When clouds appear
Like rocks and towers,
The earth's refreshed
By frequent showers.
When the wind is in the east,
It's good for neither man nor beast;
When the wind is in the north,
The fisherman he goes not forth;
When the wind is in the south,
It blows the bait in the fishes' mouth;
When the wind is in the west,
Then it's at the very best. **AT1/3b & c**

3   What does the wind make you think of as you listen to it in bed at night? **AT1/3c**

4   If the wind could be seen what sort of creature might it be? **AT1/3a & c**. Think of a gentle breeze, a strong wind or a hurricane. Follow up the discussion by drawing or painting the different creatures the wind becomes as it increases in strength. Use the Beaufort Scale in the course book as a reference. **AT2/3f**

5   Describe some of the funny sights you

have seen when the wind has made you laugh.   **AT1/3a & c**

6   How do you feel when its too rainy to play out? What are your favourite rainy day activities?   **AT1/3c**

Follow-up actvities:
1   Make a weather station. You will need a thermometer, preferably maximum and minimum, a rain gauge, and an anemometer. A barometer may be added to this basic equipment.
Keep a daily record on a classroom chart. (Science **AT9/3e**)

2   Collect the names of different types of wind e.g. tempest, cyclone, typhoon, trade wind, sirocco, simoom etc. **ATs 1-4**

Assessment Masters:
The Assessment Masters are designed as test papers. They may be used as a formal test and as such can be marked to give a percentage.

2.15a *The Birthday Party*

cloze passage — 1 mark per answer	10%	**AT2/3d**
supplying adjectives — 1 mark per answer	10%	**ATs 1-4**
Calendar — 1 marks per answer	10%	**AT2/3f**

2.15b *Flying Saucers*

comprehension passage — 3 marks per answer	15%	**AT2/3d**
past tense — 1 mark per answer	10%	**ATs 1-4**
joining sentences — 2 marks each	10%	**AT3/3a**

2.15c *A Trip in a Balloon*

letter	7%	
addressing envelope	3%	**AT3/3b-d**
description/narrative	25%	
Total	100%	

The skills breakdown is as follows:

Reading skills	35%
Writing skills	45%
Vocabulary	20%
	100%

Whether used formally or not, the Assessment Masters can establish where weaknesses lie and further practice is needed.

Suggestions for further practice:
Cloze procedure, **2.1, 2.4, 2.6, 2.7, 2.8, 2.10, 2.14**
Calendar, **1.11, 1.11a, 2.6**
months of the year, **1.11a**

Addressing an envelope, **1.3c**
Writing a letter, **2.5, 2.6**
Joining sentences:
with *and* or *but*, **1.9c, 1.17b, 2.4, 2.10, 2.10c**
with *because*, **2.5, 2.5b**
with *who* or *which*, **2.6, 2.6b**

Adjectives, **1.5a, 2.3**
Verbs, past tense, **2.6, 2.6a**

The Birthday Party

Fill in each space with a suitable word.

It was Sue's birthday. She had been sent lots of cards and had been given some very

lovely _____, but she was still disappointed. What she wanted more

_____ anything was a birthday party. All day during_____

she dreamed about having a party. When school was _____ she went

home. Her mother sent her on an _____ to the shops. She was quite a

long time_____ all the items on the list. At last she _____

home. As she opened the front door there was _____ great shout.

   'Happy Birthday!' greeted all her friends. They _____ smiling.

Behind them was a table laden with all _____ of lovely food, and in the

very middle was a birthday cake.

Copy this passage on a separate sheet of paper, changing the word *nice* for a better
describing word.

Sue had a nice time at her party. She played lots of nice games with her friends. The
birthday tea was especially nice, and the cake was the nicest she had ever had.
   At the end of the party she thanked her friends for their nice presents, the nice
cards, and for making her party so nice.
   'What a nice surprise you all gave me!' she said, 'What nice friends you all are. Now
here is a nice piece of birthday cake to take home with you.'

CALENDAR						
April						
S	M	T	W	Th	F	S
—	—	—	—	—	—	1
2	3	4	5	6	7	8
9	10	11	12	13	14	15
16	17	18	19	20	21	22
23	24	25	26	27	28	29
30	—	—	—	—	—	—

1   Sue's birthday is the third Wednesday in April.
    What date is that?_____

2   If today is the 14th —
    a)   What date will it be in one week's time?

    _____

    b)   what date will it be next Tuesday? _____

    c)   what date was it last Saturday? _____

    d)   what date was it two weeks ago? _____

2.15a   Assessment Master — cloze/adjectives/calendar
© Collins Educational 1990   AT2/3d & f; ATs 1-4

Name_____

Flying Saucers
Write all your answers on a separate sheet of paper.

Read this passage and then answer the questions.

The first flying saucer was seen in 1947. An American pilot called Kenneth Arnold saw what he described as a 'formation of nine very bright objects coming from the vicinity of Mount Baker, flying very close to the mountain tops and travelling with tremendous speed.' He described them as flying 'like a saucer would if you skipped it across the water.'

Since then thousands of people claim to have seen flying saucers. Some even say they have been kidnapped and taken on board alien space craft. Many photographs have been taken of flying saucers, but most of these are obviously fakes. Buttons have been hung on threads against the sky to look like U.F.O.'s in flight. Every year brings new reports and photographs, but no absolute proof of the existence of these space craft has ever been produced.

1 Why do you think they are called flying saucers?
2 If Kenneth Arnold did not really see flying saucers, what might he have seen?
3 Do you think it likely that people were really kidnapped by aliens?
   Say why you think so.
4 How were some photographs of U.F.O.'s faked?
5 What would prove to you that flying saucers existed?

Read this radio commentary of the sighting of flying saucers.

The flying saucers fly towards me. They shine in the sunlight. There seem to be small windows in them, but I can see nothing through them. A loud humming noise fills my ears. They hover for a moment and then move at tremendous speed. They turn, and head towards Weston Woods. They increase speed and disappear from view. The humming dies away.

Now rewrite the commentary, changing it so that it tells what has already happened. Begin like this:

The flying saucers *flew* towards me. They *shone* in the sunlight.

Joining sentences

who	which	because	and	but

Join each of these pairs of sentences, using one of the words above.

1 The flying saucer came down. It landed in a field.
2 John wanted to approach it. He was afraid.
3 He had heard about a man. The man said he had been kidnapped by aliens.
4 The man had followed a bright light. The light had led him to a flying saucer.
5 Few people believed him. He could not prove his story.

2.15b Assessment Master — comprehension/past tense/joining sentences
© Collins Educational 1990   AT2/3d; AT3/3a; ATs 1-4

A Trip in a Balloon

37 Royal Gardens,
East Marlow,
Pembury,
PB7 T1Q
12th June

Dear Pat,

I won first prize in the art competition! It's two tickets for a trip in a hot-air balloon next Saturday. Would you like to come with me? Please say you will!
We set off from the park at 2pm, weather permitting. If the wind is in the right direction we will pass right over school and then your house.
Please ask your mum and dad if you can come, and then let me know as soon as possible.
Hope to see you Saturday,
Best wishes,

CHRIS

1 On a separate sheet of paper write a reply to this letter. Say how pleased you were to hear Chris had won the competition, and thank him for his invitation. Assure him you will be there on time! Then draw an envelope outline and write Chris's address on it.

2 Write an account of your trip in the balloon. Describe what happens, what it feels like, the sounds you hear and what you see as you climb higher and higher. Say what your school and home look like as you float over them.
   Finally imagine that the weather changes suddenly and you find yourselves at the centre of a storm. Say what happens to you.

Begin like this:
  The balloon began to rise. I looked down and the people waving to us became smaller and smaller.

2.15c Assessment Master — letter/description/narrative
© Collins Educational 1990 AT3/3b-d

Pupil's Record Sheet

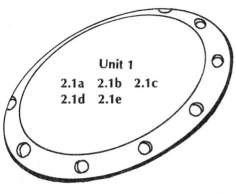

Unit 1
2.1a 2.1b 2.1c
2.1d 2.1e

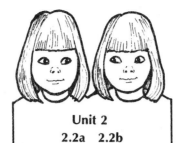

Unit 2
2.2a 2.2b
2.2c 2.2d

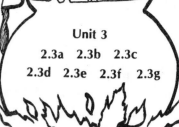

Unit 3
2.3a 2.3b 2.3c
2.3d 2.3e 2.3f 2.3g

Unit 4
2.4a 2.4b
2.4c 2.4d

Unit 5
2.5a 2.5b 2.5c
2.5d 2.5ce

Unit 6
2.6a 2.6b 2.6c 2.6d
2.6e 2.6f 2.6g 2.6h

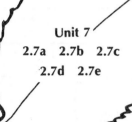

Unit 7
2.7a 2.7b 2.7c
2.7d 2.7e

Unit 8
2.8a 2.8b 2.8c 2.8d

Unit 9
2.9a 2.9b 2.9c 2.9d

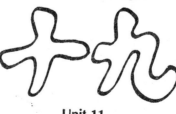

Unit 10
2.10a 2.10b 2.10c
2.10d 2.10e

Unit 11
2.11a 2.11b 2.11c

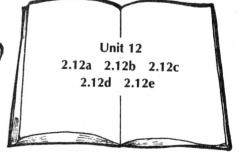

Unit 12
2.12a 2.12b 2.12c
2.12d 2.12e

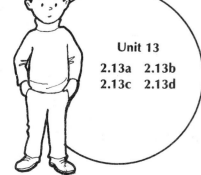

Unit 13
2.13a 2.13b
2.13c 2.13d

Unit 14
2.14a 2.14b 2.14c
2.14d 2.14e 2.14f

Unit 15
2.15a 2.15b 2.15c

English Alive Level 2	AT1 Speaking/Listening				AT2 Reading						AT3 Writing					AT4 Spelling				AT5	AT's 1-4
	a	b	c	d	a	b	c	d	e	f	a	b	c	d	e	a	b	c	d	a	
Unit 1 Pupil's Book	7		7	7		4		4	4	6	5	6 5	7 5	5 6 7	5 7				5 7	a	7
Activity Sheets	e			e				c		d	a	b e	e	c d							
Speaking/Listening Notes	6	6	3	2 3 6 7 4 5																	
Follow-up Notes				7	.8					5	7			5 6							
Unit 2 Pupil's Book	10 11		10 11			8	8	8	8 9 10 11	8	11	8	8	11 11	8	9			8		9
Activity Sheets				d			d				b						a				c
Speaking/Listening Notes	6	2	1 2 6 7 3	1 2 4 4 5 7																	3
Follow-up Notes	3		3	3								1 2		1 2			3		14		3
Unit 3 Pupil's Book			12	12		12 14 12	13 14	14 12 14	16 12 14	12	14 15	15	13 14	14 13 14	12 13 15	13 14					12 13 15
Activity Sheets			b c d e	g b c			d e d f	d e d g f g	d e g			a		c	a						a
Speaking/Listening Notes	1 3		1 3	1 2 3 4									3 4								2 3
Follow-up Notes				3										5							4
Unit 4 Pupil's Book	18		18 19	19		16 17 16 19	16 17 19	16	16 17 19	19	18 a	16			22	21			22	a e	17
Activity Sheets			a	a c d			c			a b	a c b	a b c d									
Speaking/Listening Notes	1 7		1 2 5 6 7 3 4 8 9	1 6 7 7 8 9						3 4	2 7 5 9 8 10	1 3								2 3	5
Follow-up Notes	8 9		9	6	14					5	5	22						22			21
Unit 5 Pupil's Book	21		21			20 22	22 23	24	22 23	22 23	22 23	21 23 22	22 23 22	22		22	21				21
Activity Sheets			1				c			a c b	a c b	a c b		c						a e	
Speaking/Listening Notes																					
Follow-up Notes	8	9 9	9	9					5	5	5	1 3		1 3	5				27		3
Unit 6 Pupil's Book	24		24			24	24	24	24 25 26	25 26	25 26 27	25	27	27	27	27			27	25 26	25 26
Activity Sheets		e f g	e f g h				e f	g c e h f g h	e f g h		a c	b	d	d						a	a b
Speaking/Listening Notes							1					1 5	d		5						
Follow-up Notes	4		1	1 3 5	6 1			7	7		5	1 5	9 5	5	5	5					4
Unit 7 Pupil's Book	28					28	20 22	28	26	29 30	29 30 31	30	28 31 28	27	28 31	28 31	29		28 31	a d	29
Activity Sheets											a c b	b c	c					b			a d
Speaking/Listening Notes	1 3 5 4 6 7		1 2 7 9	1 2 8 9								1 3		1 3							
Follow-up Notes	1 5		5	4								1 5 6									4

116

		a	b	c	d	a	b	c	d	e	f	a	b	c	d	e	f	a	b	c	d	e	a	b	c	d	a
Unit 8 Pupil's Book		35		35				32 33	32 33	32	32 33 34		35	35	32 33	35			35	35	35				35	34	
Activity Sheets					d			b	c	d	c									d	c	d					a b
Speaking/Listening	1	1	2 4	3	1 3				1	2	6															3	
Notes				5	2 4																						3 4
Unit 9 Pupil's Book						36 37	36 37 39	37 39	37 39	36 37	36 38	39			37	37 39		39	37 39	37 39			37 39	38			
Activity Sheets				c d	d			d			a					c											
Speaking/Listening			4	1 3	1 3											b										7 8	7 9
Notes				2 5	2 4											d											
Unit 10 Pupil's Book	42		41 42		40 41 42	41 42 43	40 41 42	40 41 43	40 41 43	43	43	40			43	43		41 42	41 42 43	41 42 43		7		43		5 23	
Activity Sheets			b c d e			b c d e	b c d e	b c e	b d e	a	a	b d				e			c	c						
Speaking/Listening	3	1 3	1 3 4	2 4	7																	8					
Notes			5 9	5	10									9	9						2 3	11				7	
Unit 11 Pupil's Book	44		44	47	44	44 45 46 47	44 46	44 46	45	50								45	45	47	45	47		47		
Activity Sheets						a	a		b c	c																
Speaking/Listening					6			6 7	6 7												8					9	
Notes					10									8	8						2 3	11					
Unit 12 Pupil's Book						48 50	48 49	48 50	48 49 50 51	50	48				48 51	48 51		48 50 51	48 51	48 50 51			48 50	48 50			
Activity Sheets			e	e				c	c	d	c					b		a b	e b	a b						
Speaking/Listening			1 2 3	3														1 2 4	2	1 2 4 5	2 6 5 7	8					
Notes					10						8																
Unit 13 Pupil's Book	52 53		52	52	52	52 54	52 54	52 53	52 53	55	55				53	53		52 53	52 53	52 53				55			
Activity Sheets	b		d		b		d	a	d	a	a					a		a b	d	c d e f	c d e f		a b d	c		
Speaking/Listening		1	1 3	d 5	6																			a	b	7 8	7 9
Notes					10						8																
Unit 14 Pupil's Book				a		56 57	56 57	57 58 59	57 58 59	55	56 57	59			59 59	58 59			61 62 64	58 59	59	55					
Activity Sheets	b		a c d e f			c d e f	c d c f	c d e f	c e	b	a	c e			c	c		b	c	b	2					
Speaking/Listening	7 8	1 7	1 3 4 5	3 6 7 8 9 1	6													7 8	7 8	2	1					5 23	
Notes																				1							
Unit 15 Pupil's Book	61	61	61		60 61 62 63	60 61 63	60 61	60 61	61 62	62 63	62 63				61 62 63 64	61 63 64 62			61 62 63 64	58 59				62		61 62 63 64	
Activity Sheets				a			a	a b	a b c	a	a				c c	b c				b	c			a b			
Speaking/Listening	4 5 2	1 3	1 2 4 5	6																							
Notes			6			4																2					

Level 2 Cassette

Side 1

Track Master Skill   *Tape Counter*

Aural memory
1   2.1e   recalling detail
            AT1/3a & d; AT3/3b-d   _____

Auditory/visual association
2   2.2d   attention to detail — matching
            spoken words to pictures
            AT1/3d; AT2/3c   _____

Handling aural information
3   2.4c   attention to detail/recording details
            on a map
            AT1/3d; AT2/3f; AT3/3c-d   _____
4   2.4d   following instructions — making a
            paper helicopter
            AT1/3d; AT3/3d   _____

Aural Memory
5   2.7e   figure/ground differentiation —
            speaker in a noisy environment
            AT1/3b   _____

Side 2
Selection
1   2.8d   using sound clues to trace route on a
            plan (zoo)
            AT1/3d; AT3/3d; AT3/3b   _____
2   2.9c   attention to detail — identifying
            places from description
            AT1/3c-d; AT3/3d   _____

Aural memory
3   2.9d   sequencing pictures from sound
            clues
            AT1/3c-d; AT2/3d   _____
4   2.12d recall of detail from an interview
            AT1/3c-d; AT3/3b   _____
5   2.13d following and retelling the words of a
            speaker
            AT1/3d; AT2/3c; AT3/3b   _____

Answer Cards for Listening Skill Masters

Teacher's Notes
When copied, these sheets may be cut up and pasted on card. This will provide an answer card for each listening skill master, allowing the children to mark their own work. Please note there is no answer card for sheet **2.4d** as this sheet is intended to be cut up and made into two helicopters.

Answers for the teacher are included in the notes for each appropriate unit.

Name _____

The Hold-Up

(Map showing: To Rifle Ridge, Nuggetville, Blood River, Echo River, Ford, Finger Rock, Echo Mountains, Prospector's Trail, Roaring Rapids, Shining Lake, Running River, Indian village, Eagle Mountains, Cave, Raging Rapids, Deadman's Trail, Blood River, Ford, Gunsmoke Gulch, Wells Fargo)

Follow-up activities

1 Nuggetville is now a ghost town. Find out what a ghost town is. Why do you think it is called Nuggetville? The name Prospector's Trail should give you a clue.

2 Write the story of the hold-up. Perhaps it does not go according to plan. Use the map to help you with your story.

3 Imagine you ride into a ghost town at dusk. Describe what you see and hear, and how you feel as the sun sets and shadows fall.

Name _____

The Real Mr. Rudge

When you know which is the real Mr. Rudge, write a description of him.

_____

_____

_____

_____

_____

_____

_____

Name _____

U.F.O.

First listen to the two eye-witness accounts on track 1, side 1 of the Level 2 listening skills cassette.

Then answer the questions below.
Each question has two answers, but only one tells what the witnesses really said.
Underline each correct answer.

1 Farmer Brown was
   a) ploughing a field
   b) mending his tractor

2 He was blinded for a moment by
   a) a bright red light
   b) a bright orange light

3 He heard a
   a) loud humming sound
   b) loud buzzing sound

4 The bright light was followed by
   a) five small red lights
   b) five small green lights

5 His feet began to
   a) tingle
   b) lift off the ground

6 The tractor began to
   a) shake
   b) lift off the ground

7 At the end
   a) he was carried off by the saucer
   b) he fell to the ground

8 P. C. Buckley was
   a) going north
   b) going south

9 P. C. Buckley said the saucer had
   a) what seemed like portholes
   b) bright, silver lights

10 The saucer was
   a) more than 25 metres in diameter
   b) less than 25 metres in diameter

Now draw what you think the saucer might have looked like.

On a separate sheet of paper tell what happened to Farmer Brown and P.C. Buckley.
Make up your own ending to the story.

Name _____

Listening

1 What did the speaker say?
a) 'McKinley has scored a goal for City!'
b) 'McKinley has scored a goal for United!'
c) 'The goal has been disallowed!'
d) 'What a goal — McKinley's done it again!'

2 What did the announcer say?
a) 'The train standing at platform 7 is running approximately ten minutes late.'
b) 'The train standing at platform 8 is about to depart.'
c) 'The train standing at platform 10 is running approximately 7 minutes late.'
d) 'The train at platform 8 is going to King's Cross.'

3 What did the secretary say?
a) 'There's a lady to see you, Miss Vines.'
b) 'There's a gentleman to see you, Mr. Vines.'
c) 'Here's your coffee, Mr. Vines.'
d) 'There are two gentlemen to see you, Miss Vines.'

4 What did the man at the bus stop say?
a) 'The number 56 bus is always late.'
b) 'The number 96 bus is never late.'
c) 'The number 96 bus is always late.'
d) 'I do wish the 56 would hurry up!'

5 What did the girl at the disco say? Are you?
a) 'I'm really thirsty. Are you?'
b) 'Do you want a drink?'
c) 'Shall we have a drink?'
d) 'Let's go and get a drink.'

6 What did the man in the garage say?
a) 'Get a move on, Joe, this tyre needs changing!'
b) 'Hurry up, Bill, this exhaust needs changing!'
c) 'Get a move on. This tyre needs changing!'
d) 'Get a move on, Mike, this tyre needs changing!'

Name _____

Using sound clues

When you have listened to the tape, and drawn the route on the map, write an account of your visit, saying something about each animal.

Name _____

Where Am I?

On the other side of this sheet write a description of two places you know well. Do not name them. See if your friend can recognise them.

Name _____

The Snatch

IMPORTANT
It is not necessary to have the actual words of Mr. Stevens,
but you should have the main details of his account.

WPC Atherton: Tell me what you can remember about the robbery.

Stevens: I was showing a young lady and gentleman a tray of diamond rings
when a man suddenly pushed between them and grabbed the tray off
the counter.

WPC Atherton: What did the man look like?

Stevens: He was wearing blue jeans and a red sweater.

WPC Atherton: Did he say anything?

Stevens: No, he just grabbed the tray and ran out of the shop. He bumped into
a lady at the door and knocked her to the floor.

WPC Atherton: What happened then?

Stevens: Miss Spencer helped the lady to her feet and I ran into the High
Street after the thief.

WPC Atherton: Did you see which way he went?

Stevens: Oh, yes. He was running hell for leather up the street and I set off
after him, shouting 'Stop, thief!'. He turned up an alley, but when I
got there he was gone.

WPC Atherton: What did you do then?

Stevens: I came back to the shop and phoned you.

WPC Atherton: What was the value of the rings?

Stevens: About £7,000.

On a separate sheet of paper write a similar interview with a woman who witnessed a
road accident.

Name _____

Chit-Chat interviews Jason Lee

First listen to the interview on track 4, side 2
of the Level Two listening skills cassette.
Then answer the questions below.
Each question has three answers, but only
one of them tells what Jason Lee really said.
Underline each correct answer.

1 When did Jason Lee first decide to be an athlete?
   a) at primary school
   b) at secondary school
   c) at university

2 Over which distance did he win the Olympic gold medal?
   a) 1 500 metres
   b) 800 metres
   c) 3 000 metres

3 Who at primary school sometimes beat him?
   a) Christopher Mills
   b) John Appleton
   c) Lee Mills

4 Over which distance could the Olympic champion always win at primary school?
   a) 100 metres
   b) 800 metres
   c) 200 metres

5 Who organised his training?
   a) himself
   b) his teacher
   c) his father

6 Where did his training take place?
   a) in the country
   b) in the park
   c) at school

7 Was his school work affected?
   a) he didn't think so
   b) it was
   c) definitely not

8 What did Jason Lee say a runner needed, besides strong legs?
   a) powerful arms
   b) an active brain
   c) expensive running shoes

Use the information on this sheet to write an article about Jason Lee for *Chit-Chat*
magazine.

Name _____

Off to the Beach

What do you think Carl is dreaming of?
Do you ever have dreams when you look up at the sky?
Write your answers on the other side of this sheet.

Adventures in English

Adventures in English is a series of computer programs for the BBC Micro. Each program comes complete with an accompanying Pressure-fax book of spiritmaster activity sheets which reinforce the learning objectives. There is an adventure to complement each full-format book of the *English Alive* course.

The adventure programs develop logical thought and problem solving skills. By creating situations which stretch the pupils' imagination and take them beyond everyday experiences, they will provide the stimulus for a wide variety of follow-up work across the curriculum. A chart on page 121 shows the skills targeted for each program.

Spellbound is the adventure which links with Level 2.

In addition to these adventures are two further programs available on one disc: *What is a Sentence?* and *Some Common Confusions*. They are ideal remedial aids for teaching essential, basic sentence construction and to distinguish between homophones. These programs do not have an accompanying Pressure-fax book.

Spellbound

Unit 3 of Book 2 provides the ideal introduction to *Spellbound*, the third in the *Adventures in English* series.

Spellbound consists of a computer program and a Pressure-fax book of 24 activity sheets. The children are imprisoned in the castle of the evil witch, Grizelda, and have to solve many problems before they can escape. The program helps with phonic work, word recognition and the development of vocabulary skills.

The Pressure-fax book is divided into four sections.

Sheets 1-3 are designed for use with the computer program to record progress. (See program notes.)

Sheets 4-8 develop further the skills needed in the computer program. All the questions in this section are similar in style to those in the program.

Sheets 9-18 widen the scope to include further vocabulary and spelling work, dictionary work and sentence sequencing.

Sheets 19-23 introduce comprehension and creative writing and lead on to more open-ended activities. The theme of magic and witchcraft is maintained throughout these worksheets, giving opportunities for creative writing, drama, dance, and art and craft. The final sheet (24) gives a number of such ideas for children to develop.

1 **Spellbound** — the program 1
2 **Spellbound** — the program 2
3 **Spellbound** — the program 3
4 **The Torn Message** (sentence rearrangement) **AT3/3a**
5 **Ten More Locked Doors** (spelling) **AT4/3a-b**
6 **Two Towers** (sentences/odd man out) **AT3/3e; ATs 1-4**
7 **Two More Towers** (cloze procedure/ spelling/vocabulary) **AT2/3d; AT4/3a**
8 **The Torn Notice** (cloze procedure) **AT2/3d**
9 **Word Search** (spelling) **ATs 1-4**
10 **Word Steps** (dictionary work/spelling) **ATs 1-4; AT2/3d & f**
11 **Grizelda's Maze** (vocabulary) **AT2/3f; ATs 1-4**
12 **Word Web** (spelling/vocabulary) **ATs 1-4; AT4/4a-b**
13 **Witch's Tale** (sentence completion) **AT3/3a-c**
14 **Word Ladder** (dictionary work/ sentence sequencing) **AT2/3c & f**
15 **Spells and Spelling** (dictionary work/ spelling) **ATs 1-4; AT2/3f; AT3/3e**
16 **More Spells** (spelling) **AT4/3a-b**
17 **Witch's Brew** (vocabulary/spelling) **AT2/3d; AT3/3d**
18 **Prisoners in the Witch's Orchard** (spelling/sentence sequencing) **ATs 1-4; AT3/3c**
19 **Grizelda's Map** (map work/ comprehension) **AT2/3d; AT3/3d**
20 **Grizelda's Picture Gallery** — 1 (creative drawing)
21 **Grizelda's Picture Gallery** — 2 (creative drawing)
22 **The Cottage in the Wood** (comprehension/writing/ drawing) **AT2/3d; AT3/3b-d**
23 **How to Make a Broomstick Fly** (cloze procedure/verse) **AT2/3d; AT3/3b**
24 **Witchcraft** (creative writing/drama/ art/craft) **AT3/3b-c; AT1/3d**

Spellbound and the National Curriculum

The chart below shows how *Spellbound* integrates with the National Curriculum.

This page may be photocopied and used as a pupil's record sheet. Details may then be transferred to any pupil's profile.

ENGLISH KEY STAGE 1, LEVEL 3								
Attainment Target	**Description**	***Spellbound* references**						
AT1	c) Listen and respond	Program						
	d) Instructions	Program,	24					
AT2	c) Listen, discuss, recall	14	24					
	d) Inference, deduction	7	8	10	17	19	22	23
	f) Select/use information	10	11	14	15	17		
AT3	a) Independent writing	4	13					
	b) Chronological writing	13	22	23				
	c) More complex stories	13	18	22	24			
	d) Non-chronological writing	19						
	e) Begin to revise, redraft	6	15					
AT4	a) Spell simple words	5	7	12	16			
	b) Regular patterns	5	12	16				
AT's 1–4	Word skills	6	9	10	11	12	15	18

Name _____

Date begun _____ Date completed _____

Comments _____

_____

_____

_____

Teacher _____

Adventures in English Skills Chart with National Curriculum Attainment Targets and Levels

Book ▲
Program ●
Book and Program ○

AT1 Speaking & Listening

	Goblin Winter (Level 2)	Spooky Towers (Level 3)	Spellbound (Level 4)	Pirate's Treasure (Level 4)	Wreckers' Rock (Level 5)	McGinty's Gold (Level 5)	Common Confusions (Levels 3-5)	What is a Sentence? (Levels 3-5)
follow story and recall	●							
listen in discussion	●	●	●	●	●	●		
drama	▲	▲	▲	▲	▲	▲		
discuss constructively	●	●	●	●	●	●		

AT2 Reading

	Goblin Winter (Level 2)	Spooky Towers (Level 3)	Spellbound (Level 4)	Pirate's Treasure (Level 4)	Wreckers' Rock (Level 5)	McGinty's Gold (Level 5)	Common Confusions (Levels 3-5)	What is a Sentence? (Levels 3-5)
reading with understanding	▲	▲	▲	○	○	○		
directions and instructions						○		
fact and opinion						▲		
inferences and predictions						▲		
cloze procedure	▲	▲	○	○	▲			
where to look					○	▲		
dictionary work			▲	▲	▲			
telephone directories					○			
timetables					○			
instructions					▲	▲		
maps			▲	▲	○	○		
atlas					▲			
encyclopedia					▲	▲		
reference library				▲	▲	▲		
other sources						▲		

AT3 Writing

	Goblin Winter (Level 2)	Spooky Towers (Level 3)	Spellbound (Level 4)	Pirate's Treasure (Level 4)	Wreckers' Rock (Level 5)	McGinty's Gold (Level 5)	Common Confusions (Levels 3-5)	What is a Sentence? (Levels 3-5)
finishing a sentence		▲						
capital letters/full stops		○						●
making complete sense		○						●
question sentences								●
matching questions/answers					▲			
exclamations								●
mixed-up sentences		▲						
sentence sequencing	▲	▲	▲	▲				
joining sentences						▲		
correcting sentences						▲		
the apostrophe						▲		
direct and indirect speech						▲		
2/3 sentence stories	▲	▲						
3/6 sentence stories	▲	▲						
longer stories	▲	▲	▲	▲	▲	▲		
descriptions				▲	▲	▲		
letters						▲		
"telegram" stories						▲		
headline stories						▲		
recording events					▲	▲		
writing in paragraphs						▲		
verse					▲			
directions and instructions						▲		
writing to suit reader						▲		
explaining processes						▲		
making notes						▲		

ATs1-4 Knowledge about language

	Goblin Winter (Level 2)	Spooky Towers (Level 3)	Spellbound (Level 4)	Pirate's Treasure (Level 4)	Wreckers' Rock (Level 5)	McGinty's Gold (Level 5)	Common Confusions (Levels 3-5)	What is a Sentence? (Levels 3-5)
nouns		▲						
verbs		▲		○				
adjectives		▲						
adverbs						▲		
pronouns						▲		
prepositions		▲						
alphabetical order	▲	▲			▲			
colours	○							
consonants and vowels	○	○						
comparisons	○	▲						
singular and plural	▲	▲						
families	▲							
homes	▲							
occupations	▲							
gender	▲							
groups and collections						▲		
containers				▲				
classification				▲				
sounds			○					
antonyms			○					
synonyms						▲		
homophones							●	
rhymes	○	○		▲				
right word in right place	○	○	○	○				
odd man out		▲	○	▲				
word ladders			▲					
word search/recognition		▲	▲	▲				
making words from letters			▲	▲				
word building	○							
correcting spellings		▲						
crosswords			○	○				
anagrams	●	○	○	○				
other word puzzles				▲	○	○		

Cross-curricular

	Goblin Winter (Level 2)	Spooky Towers (Level 3)	Spellbound (Level 4)	Pirate's Treasure (Level 4)	Wreckers' Rock (Level 5)	McGinty's Gold (Level 5)	Common Confusions (Levels 3-5)	What is a Sentence? (Levels 3-5)
Dance	▲							
Art and Craft	▲	▲	▲	▲	▲	▲		
Music	▲							
Cookery	▲							
Topic Work and Projects	▲	▲	▲	▲	▲	▲		

Level 2: Index

Suffixes: **a, b, c, d, e** etc. indicate **Activity Masters**. **N** indicates **Teacher's Notes**
This index also includes Skillmasters from Level 1.

126